P

PROMOTED

Bozi Dar is a rarity. A bona fide top performer with the curiosity and self-awareness to pinpoint exactly what he's doing that works. If you're eager to get ahead and want insights that will catapult you to the top of your profession, you need to read this book.

~ Ron Friedman, Ph.D.,
Author of The Best Place to Work: The Art and
Science of Creating an Extraordinary Workplace

Bozi's got one of the best formulas for fast career acceleration out there. I know traditional, conventional job advice doesn't work anymore because the world's changing. Career advice has to change, too. PROMOTED is out-right one of the best systems I've seen for getting unstuck. The best part is you're not working harder, you don't have to be the first one in the office and the last to leave.

~Joshua Waldman
Author of Job Searching with Social Media For Dummies,
Founder of CareerEnlightenment.com an award winning career blog

I've always had an unconventional outlook on my career, so when I first heard about Bozi Dar's Career Acceleration Formula and PRO-MOTED, I knew I was going to be a fan. And boy was that true. His advice is so unlike any I've ever come across, but it completely resonates with me. I know what it's like to bounce around looking for the right career, but when you find that special edge that sets you apart, it's magic. This book is perfect for anyone who is feeling stagnant in their career and needs that boost, almost giving them permission to be awesome. I highly recommend it as a way to be able to follow a clear cut path AND set yourself apart from everyone else who isn't getting the results they want in their career. Even better than all of this I have per-

sonally used some of the strategies that Bozi describes in this book to get promoted and raises many multiple times over... so I know it works!"

~**Scott Barlow** - Founder & CEO,
Happen To Your Career

Bozi Dar's PROMOTED is a game changer. Bozi provides tried and tested system that you can use both now and any time in the future to grow your career fast, without working until midnight or following the game of office politics. Every ambitious professional should have this book on their bookshelf and read it over and over.

~**Kevin Kermes:**
Founder of All Things Career

I run into people all the time who are feeling stuck in their job, and are looking for that one thing that can set them apart and make them stand out from the competition. PROMOTED by Bozi Dar is a book that anyone who is looking to take their career to the next level should read. Bozi's Career Acceleration Formula is going to make someone feel uncomfortable, but any change is going to be uncomfortable. The trade-off is going to be a career that someone's only ever dreamed of. Don't waste any more time on advice from "experts" who are just re-hashing the same story... pick up PROMOTED and get ready to see some dramatic results in your own career.

~**Lisa Rangel**
Managing Director, Chameleon Resumes

Every day I work with job seekers, helping them find their ideal career path, so over the years I've come across a lot of advice. Bozi's advice stands out and the results of his students are dramatic. If you are looking for that "secret sauce" on how to leapfrog your competition, then do yourself a favor and read PROMOTED.

~**Alan Carniol**
Founder, Interview Success Formula

PROMOTED

THE PROVEN CAREER ACCELERATION FORMULA TO REACH THE TOP WITHOUT WORKING HARDER OR PLAYING OFFICE POLITICS

Bozi Dar

ABOUT THE AUTHOR

Bozi Dar is a senior executive and trusted career advisor to Fortune 500 professionals. After struggling to advance his own career for years, he discovered a simple, 6-step system, which helped him land six job promotions in six years, with a 15x increase in salary. Over the years, he refined and perfected his system based on his actual corporate experience (no fluff and no theory), helping thousands of ambitious professionals to consistently score a job promotion fast and launch a super-successful career that 90% of people will never experience in their lifetime.

Bozi's personal story goes back in 2005, when he spent the first three years of his corporate career working in an entry-level sales job, struggling to make a decent living and getting passed over again and again for job promotions by others who were not really more qualified than him. After changing companies and still having the same abysmal results, he did something radical.

He quit his job and spent the next 12 months trying to figure out what went wrong, and come up with his strategies for career success, with the goal of getting 5x results in half of the time (what Bozi calls the "10x effect"). After much introspection and analysis, his path became crystal clear. He knew exactly the company he wanted to work for and the path he would take to get there, so he put his strategies to the test.

The results were a meteoric rise up the corporate ladder, and within six years he was promoted six times, increased his salary 15x, and managed a $5 billion product portfolio. Along the way, people were noticing his success, not only his bosses, but also his peers and colleagues. He became highly sought after for career advice by others wanting to learn his secrets so they could duplicate his success. Over time, Bozi was coaching more and more people, teaching his strategies until he perfected his 6-step Career Acceleration Formula.

Today, Bozi's Career Acceleration Formula is used by thousands of achievers from 20+ countries, working for companies like Google, Cisco, Ford, Siemens, JP Morgan, Oracle, Ralph Lauren, Johnson + Johnson, and many others.

CONTENTS

Chapter 1

A NEW STRATEGY FOR A NEW CAREER WORLD

Ten years ago, on a beautiful summer afternoon, two young men graduated from the same business school. These two young men were very much alike; both had been excellent students, were charismatic and, as young business school graduates tend to be, were filled with ambitious dreams for their futures. Both wanted to work in the field of marketing at a Fortune 500 technological company, become rising stars, and secure a global manager role within seven years.

Recently, these two men reconnected on LinkedIn. After some correspondence, they agreed to meet for dinner to catch up after ten years.

After ten years they were still very much alike. Both were happily married. Both had bought a house. And both, it turned out, had started to work in their dream position: a marketing role at a Fortune 500 technological company, and were still there.

But there was one difference. One of them was a manager of a small department in their company, the other was a vice president.

One of them had ended up where 90% of corporate professionals end up, while the other had entered, what I call, the 10% club.

What Made The Difference

I used to wonder, as I'm sure you do from time to time, what makes this kind of difference in people's lives?

It isn't intelligence or talent or dedication. It isn't that one person wants success and the other doesn't.

And in my experience it isn't luck.

No, what I've found is the difference lies in the strategy that each person decides to follow in their career; a conventional strategy vs. an unconventional strategy.

Early in my own career I followed a conventional career strategy, but the moment I started applying an unconventional strategy, the game changed for me.

I'll share more details later in the book, but here are just a couple of things that changed for me: by using the hidden job market I got a dream job position that wasn't open yet, I ended up getting nominated for a national award, and got promoted six times in six years, with my salary being 15 times more than what I'd started out with. Pretty amazing results, right?

Soon people started to come to me for career advice, and I realized there was nothing out there based on what I'd done. Most career advice out there was based on traditional strategies, which got you traditional results.

I knew something had to change.

That's why I put together the book you're holding in your hands. That's why I put together Promoted: The Career Acceleration Formula To Reach The Top Without Working Harder Or Playing Office Politics.

For that's the whole purpose of the formula: to provide you with an unconventional strategy to get you the career results you desire.

A Career Strategy Unlike Any Other

You see, this book offers you a unique career acceleration strategy (which I often refer to as the Career Acceleration Formula). It's the only strategy that promises to get you promoted within 6 to 12 months, based on the experience of hundreds of my students. It's the only strategy out there that's helped unemployed graduates get their dream job AND helped grizzled corporate veterans to reignite their career.

Would you like to make $10,000 more next year? How about $20,000…. $30,000? Doing so is a piece of cake once you join the 10% club, which is something you'll learn about later and which I'll show you how to join.

Do you wish to be mentored by VPs, CEOs and ex-CEOs? This isn't hard once you learn how to use your One Big Thing to become the center of influence, something you'll learn about in Chapter 6. I've seen students go from being an anonymous cog to being an autonomous leader in their organization because they have the trust of senior management.

Do you want to have hiring managers and top recruiters fight over you? Throwing more money than you know what to do with and insane perks to win you over to their division? This becomes automatic once you learn how to make your boss work for you, something I talk about in Chapter 7.

The best thing? You don't need to be a sleazy networker.

I'm not a big fan of the word "networking," I prefer to think about it in terms of the authentic and genuine connections I want to make. Some of the best mentors I've had throughout my career are still my friends today. Conventional career advice is to play office politics. I'll show you how to be honest, professional, and get dramatic results in your "network."

Will this require you to work hard? To put in all-nighters and work weekends? No. You will still need to put in the work to get results, but all of my students learn one thing when they start out: *work smart, not hard.* In order to begin, all I ask is for you to spend 10 minutes at the start of your day to work on your career. 10 minutes. That's the time it takes to make two cups of coffee.

Can you afford to spend 10 minutes a day to get promoted in 12 months?

Just in case you think this is all luck, throughout this book you'll learn more about my story and the stories of some of my students. I won't lie; I'm proud of my students, and you'll hear me brag about them often. But over the years, I've helped hundreds of ambitious professionals get promoted and get their career back on track. I've distilled it down to a formula, a step-by-step strategy that uses timeless, yet proven, principles. It worked a hundred years ago, and it'll work for decades to come.

So the choice is up to you. You can continue to be bored every day in your job, to get passed over for a promotion time after time, while your colleagues and managers take the credit for YOUR hard work. You can worry about bills and your financial future, getting a meager 2% annual salary rise while your bills go up by 5% every year. You can continue to be anonymous, getting the low visible projects that ensure you continue to be forgotten in the organization, while seeing your peers get promoted and realize dramatic results in their careers.

Or you can decide, right now, to take action. To change your situation. To not procrastinate anymore about your career and *hope* that you'll finally land that promotion you've been working for over the years, but instead to find your perfect job role and to take massive action to get it within 6 to 12 months.

Back to those two business school classmates I mentioned at the beginning of this chapter. They graduated from the same business school and started their careers working in the same role. So what made their career path different?

The strategy they chose. A conventional strategy got the conventional results. An unconventional strategy got the unconventional results.

Which strategy will you choose?

What's Coming Up Next

So what can you expect in this book? In this first chapter you'll get introduced to the big picture and how the world is changing. You'll learn how corporations are coping with the change, and why the turmoil and chaos means that the old, unwritten contract of job security is dead. You'll learn why entering the 10% club is the only way to be immune from market conditions, and just what traits companies are on the lookout for in order to survive. You'll learn that while this turmoil is bad for organizations, it also presents opportunities for professionals like you, professionals who are willing to enter the 10% club.

After that you'll be introduced to my story of how I got fired from my first job and then turned my life and career around to getting promoted six times in six years, increasing my salary 15x and landing a senior role where I managed portfolio of products worth $5 billion. You'll also learn the story of how I started mentoring other students, which led me to create the Career

Acceleration Formula, a step-by-step system that's helped hundreds of students achieve the career success they've always desired. Finally, you'll be introduced to the 6-step formula and how it all fits together, and what you can expect from the rest of the book. As you go through each step of the formula, you'll be introduced to some of my students, and learn how they've used that particular step to revolutionize their careers.

As you go through this book, think of me as a trusted mentor. At times I'll point out to you what you've been doing wrong, and I'll shatter some of your most cherished beliefs. It may seem tough, but that's what a mentor is for: to pull you through the painful moments so you can get the results you desire. I'll ask you to keep moving forward because I assure you, no matter what your career problem is, the seeds of the solution lie somewhere inside this book.

All right, let's learn about how and why the world is changing, and how you can take advantage of that to radically alter the direction of your career.

THE CAREER WORLD IS RAPIDLY CHANGING

It's never been easier for a company to get knocked out of the top.

Over a thousand years ago, your only chance of being a billionaire and being able to influence world markets was to be born into royalty or nobility. Your only other chance was to be an individual like Marcus Licinius Crassus of Rome, the only private citizen with an unprecedented amount of personal wealth in his time, who had to resort to mass execution, forceful seizure of land, trading in slaves, and other questionable practices to build his wealth and rule Rome. One thousand years later, the rise of the industrial revolution and capitalism allowed wealth to be placed in the hands of private individuals via more ethical means, as in the well-known case of J.D. Rockefeller. Except, it took him 20 years to build his fortune.

The pace of technological disruption in the past two decades means that companies and individuals are reaching these levels of wealth incomparably faster. Just think of the two Stanford University PhD students who went from forming a company called Google in their garage, to accomplishing unquantifiable success only six years later. Or think about a more recent startup, Uber, which is disrupting taxi services worldwide and reached the value of $50 billion in only five years' time!

Companies are being disrupted faster and faster. Today, we see these kind of abrupt changes happening every day.

Fifty years ago the lifespan of a Fortune 500 company was 75 years. Today, it's less than 15 years.

That means during the time of the baby boomers, if you got employed at a Fortune 500 company, you didn't need to worry about your employer going out of business. Security was guaranteed. You knew the company was going to outlast you.

Today, if a Fortune 500 company employs you, a startup company that is going to put your employer out of business could be launched tomorrow. This disruptive environment makes everyone uncertain about the future. And companies that are uncertain about the future don't have the foresight to invest in their employees.

It's expected that, at the current churn rate of companies, 75% of the S&P 500 will be replaced by 2027.

In 12 years, your employers might be the entrepreneurs who are just now entering university.

No Matter Who You Are, Automation And Outsourcing Is Threatening Your Job

On top of all this, your job might not even exist in the future. By 2050, it is estimated that machines and computers will do 50% of today's jobs.

Only 10 years ago, being a Black Cab driver in London was a safe and pretty lucrative job. To qualify for it, the drivers were required to pass a test for which it took them 2-4 years to prepare, and which resulted in real, physical changes in their brain; their grey matter got redistributed in the process of learning and acquiring new skills. And now, two simple technological advancements that aren't that groundbreaking relative to other technological breakthroughs, GPS and smartphones, mean that an enterprise that's been around for over 900 years is at risk of becoming extinct.

And it's not just London. Uber is already available in 300 other cities. You might be sitting there thinking that your industry isn't going to befall the same fate. Computers and artificial intelligence are, after all, still far from replacing human beings in the majority of jobs. So you might feel secure and confident that your job isn't going to get farmed out to a software lab somewhere, and that a demand for your role, requiring years of acquiring specific skills and expertise, will always be there.

Unfortunately, employment data from 20 countries shows that in the past four years, software has been replacing the middle class at an alarming rate, lawyers, architects, even doctors, no one's job is secure anymore.

The Unwritten Job Contract Is Dead

All this means that the unwritten contract that existed between your parents and their employers is dead. The agreement went like this: Work for us every day, do a good job, and you'll be employed for life and have a pension for retirement. Yet this contract is no more. The rise of automation, globalization, and increasing technological disruption means your employer could go out of business tomorrow. Just ask Lehman Brothers or Blockbuster. Your employer isn't faithful to you. They simply can't afford to be.

The unwritten contract is dead. It's time to take your career into your own hands.

Say goodbye to job security. Being a good employee and doing good work is not enough to keep your job.

In the past, it was considered a risk to speak out, to be a disruptive employee, to break the rules, as that behavior led to unemployment. Now do you know what's risky? Playing it safe, not taking a chance to try out a new strategy, and continuing to be an average employee. That's the kind of behavior which makes you easily replaceable.

THE INVISIBLE FORCES THAT HOLD YOU BACK

Let's get something straight. It's not your fault that you're struggling to get promoted. The real reason that you're being held back is because you've been given crappy career advice all your life.

Think about it: You navigate one of the most important areas of your life, your career, based on the advice that you get. You read a few articles and ask people what you should do, and then apply their advice. Yet you never ask yourself whether the people behind the advice have the same goals and priorities that you have, or what is incentivizing them.

Stop for a minute and open your mind to the possibility that everything you've learned up till now about career advancement could be just plain wrong.

What you'll read below will make you feel uncomfortable. However, I invite you to push beyond that feeling, as what you'll learn will pay off dividends in the future. Remember, unconventional thinking brings unconventional results.

Let's look at the underlying motivations from the usual sources of career advice:

Family and Friends: You would think that your family and friends have your best interests at heart and want you to succeed. They do. But at the same time, subconsciously, they want something else for you, as well. Your family members, for example, prioritize your safety and security, so their advice will come from one place: Keeping you safe. Your friends, on the other hand, even though this may not be their conscious choice, don't want you to change too much. Change can be scary. People tend to feel the need to hold onto the familiar. If you change, even if it's to grow, your friendship might not survive. Just ask friends of lottery winners. This is why your friends will give you the type of advice that conforms to their internal needs.

The Internet: Usually it makes sense to look for help online. This way you can get advice from experts, which you can apply immediately to your own career. No doubt they have your best interests at heart, right? Well, they don't. These websites win when they keep you confused. This keeps up their page views, which raises their advertising revenues, their main source of income. To summarize, the more confused you are about how to advance in your career, the more money the websites and blogs make.

Career Coaches: Surely then, you'll say, it must be beneficial to get direct, one-on-one help with a career coach? Well, yes. Until you start to look at their pricing model, as most charge by the hour. It's naturally in their interest to charge you for more sessions (ranging from $200 to $500 per session), which means it's not in their interest to give you clear actionable information in your first session. Besides, you ought to assess their expertise first. Have these coaches experienced rapid career progress *themselves*?

Your Organization: Finally, your organization seems like the most logical place for career advice, as they know what's best for each role in their organization, and your success should be their success. Until you begin to realize that your company hierarchy is set out like a pyramid - with a limited amount of senior positions for an abundance of talent. The organization's priority is to retain all this talent while keeping this workforce asset ticking over. This is why they set arbitrary "checkboxes" required for you to move up the corporate ladder. These so-called "requirements" have nothing to do with whether you'll be competent at a desired role or not. In other words, your organization essentially doesn't care about you; they care about themselves.

WHY THE ODDS ARE STACKED AGAINST YOU

So let's tally all this up:

- Technological disruption means that your company might not be around tomorrow.
- In the future, chances are that your job is going to be replaced with a computer or a machine, or outsourced to countries where labor is cheaper.

- The old, unwritten contract where you exchange company loyalty for security is broken.
- Most of the advice you're given to help you with your career is plain wrong.

The environment you're in is set up for you to lose, and you're being given advice that does more harm than good. It's no wonder that you're not advancing in your career!

In other words, the odds are stacked against you.

All these changes in the job market may cause you to feel uncertain about your career. Uncertainty, when out of control, can seriously harm your progress.

When you're uncertain about your career, when you feel that the floor underneath you is something you can't rely on, you find it impossible to make plans. You enter into a scarcity mindset. In this scarcity mindset, the last thing on your mind is to take risks, to go against the status quo.

When you're uncertain about your career, that uncertainty affects your whole life. You don't know if you'll have a job a year from now, which means you feel anxious about big spending commitments, like paying the deposit on your house or paying for your college tuition. You even avoid making sensible investment decisions for your retirement.

It used to be enough to be loyal and hardworking. A few decades ago that would have given you job security.

Today, that's not enough.

In today's world, the real job security comes from having a set of skills and a strategy that will allow you to stay in the 10% club, independent of the economy and independent of the future of the organization your work for. A strategy that is based on timeless principles. A strategy that will give you an unfair advantage in this new career world. That's what my Career Acceleration Formula is, in its essence.

If you don't start learning and applying the new strategy, you will end up trapped in the 90% crowd. You will be like Blockbuster, not seeing the writing on the wall.

Here is what happens to employees who don't understand this and end up trapped in the 90% crowd. They:

- Wake up going to work feeling tired, undervalued and under-appreciated at work.
- Never get recognized for their contributions to the company, and when they do something worthy of recognition, someone else takes the credit.
- Feel like their career is stagnating while their peers get promoted ahead of them for significant job positions.
- Feel like a total failure, not only to their ambition, but to their family who believed in them and to their friends who saw their true potential.
- Feel a profound sense of failure at not fulfilling their potential if they've turned 65 and never left the 90% crowd. Deep inside they know they've let themselves down.

THE NEW WORLD OF CAREER OPPORTUNITIES

Clearly we live in disruptive times. But change isn't all-bad.

Yes, businesses are being disrupted and there are new players coming into the market, however, not everyone loses in this game. The 90% crowd gets fired when the company needs to downsized, but the 10% club get promoted, are given a new area of responsibility, and a large pay rise.

But these circumstances are also a tremendous source of opportunity. With such massive pressures from the market, companies that want to get ahead need people now more than ever who can not only deliver results, but can also take charge of their career.

Do you know what one of the biggest worries of CEOs is? Managing talent. Specifically, retaining and hiring top talent. Not just for technical roles, but also for leadership roles. Companies are finding it hard to find the correct talent with leadership capabilities to guide their divisions in this brave new world. *"The year-to-year consistency in our findings tells us that future leadership, or lack thereof, is top of mind for organizations nearly everywhere,"* a senior HR Consultant described.

Companies are not only finding it hard to identify talent they need within their ranks, but the few they have are vanishing, they are being snatched by their competitors. Your organization needs now, more than ever, talented leaders to guide them through the problems of tomorrow. If you feel you are ready to be one of those leaders, in return they will reward you with more responsibility, giving you more exposure, and the opportunity for your career to accelerate.

I don't need to mention that this increased responsibility will come with a much bigger paycheck.

All you need is the right strategy, and the opportunities will all start to come your way.

Do You Leverage The Hidden Job Market?

You might think, "Hang on, I know companies need talent to help them in this new world, but why do all the job positions seem to be taken?" Well, I've got news for you. **Seventy percent of job positions are hidden (this number goes up to 80% for executive jobs).**

What do I mean by *hidden*? I mean they are filled without being advertised. How? And more importantly, why? Why do companies fill these positions without advertising them?

Think about it from the company's perspective. It takes months to flesh out and justify the need for a new position. The proposal then is discussed at senior levels, and if it's approved, is accounted for in the budget.

After the new position has been approved, the first thing that happens is the, "Who do you know?" stage. Word is put out to the company employees to find someone in their network to fill the position. It's cheaper for the company to work through a referral than to pay for advertising or for an expensive recruiter. On top of this, the chances are that, if it comes through your employee's network, the new employee will be a good fit for the company culture. Also, if it is your top talent referring someone for the position, there's a chance the referral is just as talented.

If this process fails to produce a candidate, then the next stage is to offer a monetary incentive to employees to find someone to fill the position. This still ends up being cheaper than advertisements or involving recruiters.

By this point, 70% of job positions are filled.

Only then do the final 30% of jobs get advertised or sent to recruiters.

Chances are if the jobs haven't been filled by this time, they are the most undesirable jobs.

In other words, when you respond to jobs via ads or by working through recruiters, you are applying for the bottom 30% of jobs. Oh, and guess what? Everyone else is applying for that job, too.

In fact, guess who are the only people who aren't applying for that job? The 10% club.

Think about that: 90% of employees are applying for 30% of the jobs, while 10% are getting 70% of the jobs.

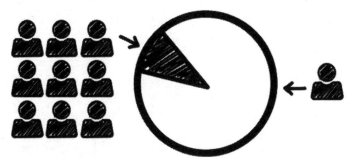

Figure 1: *Which sounds better? Being the 90% that compete for 30% of the jobs or being the 10% that are getting 70% of the jobs.*

What's more, there are so many jobs in the hidden job market, that *you don't even need to compete,* because you are either applying for an unannounced position, or, even better, **you create your own job role**. The only person you are competing against there is yourself. You're playing a game where you write the rules.

This is the critical secret to the 10% club.

Which group would you rather be in, the 10% club or the 90% crowd?

The good news for you is that it's easier than ever before to be in the 10% club, especially because of all the bad career advice that everyone else is soaking up.
In fact, by changing just *a few* of your strategies, you can catapult yourself into this extraordinarily successful club.

One of my early mentors once told me something that I've used throughout my career, *"If you are failing to achieve the results you want, it just means that you don't have the right information."*

So, how did I find the right information? How did I design the strategy I'm going to share with you in this book that got me promoted six times in six years?

To share that, I first have to tell you about a young ambitious professional at the start of his career…

FROM BEING FIRED TO BEING HIRED LIKE A VIP

I couldn't believe it. In two years, I'd gone from being fired because of office politics to being driven around in a black limousine to interview for a job position that wasn't even open yet.

Let me back up a bit.

After doing exceedingly well in college, I got a job doing entry-level sales in the healthcare industry. Within three months, I was on top of the board, the best man in my team. I was a rising star. Success was mine.

Or so I thought.

Due to some office politics and mistakes on how I handled the situation, I got fired. You'll learn more about this in the next chapter, but this incident taught me a lesson that would help me in my career.

Let me tell you, as a young man in his first job, getting fired really sucks. It not only affects your income, but it destroys your self-confidence.

For this reason, I took a year off to try and gather my wits together and recharge. I went back into academia and started to analyze what I did wrong, and in my pursuit of answering this question (and after reading a shit load of books), I began to form this idea of 10x thinking: What can I do in my career to get 10x results?

When it came time for me to find my next job, I decided to go against common wisdom and do something a bit radical and different.

I was a bit apprehensive, but I knew I had nothing to lose. Within a few weeks, something amazing happened.

*I was standing outside my house with a black BMW waiting to drive me to an interview for a job position **that wasn't even open yet**.*

Here I was, a business student, barely able to afford his own groceries, and I was getting VIP treatment.

That's when the penny dropped. That's when I knew I was entering the 10% club, and life would never be the same for me again.

Suffice it to say, I got the job. Over the following years I refined and improved on the strategies that I'll teach you in the book, which led to me getting promoted six times in six years with a 15x bump in salary. In the next chapter, I'll reveal the whole journey I went through to achieve that success. You'll see how you can rise from any situation and turn total failure to complete success. Trust me, it'll be worth it.

Sometimes I wonder, if I'd listened to all the traditional advice, applied to job boards and submitted my resume to several companies instead of using my 10x career strategies, would I have gotten that VIP treatment?

Most likely not. And that's why you need a new strategy. That's why you need my Career Acceleration Formula that I present in this book.

5 THINGS TO EXPECT ON YOUR PROMOTION JOURNEY

What can you expect to face on this journey of rapid career advancement? Well, here are the five things that you're going to face:

#1 Results

If you take action based on the principles I'll share in this book, you're going to start getting results, and you're going to get them fast.

I personally believe that talk is cheap, which is why I'm going to show you how to get results in the quickest manner possible, and guide you through the process of how to land that promotion and create your perfect career.

Think about that for a second: You'll get a new job title within 12 months. How much would it be worth to you to get moving in your career again?

You'll also start to see results in the opportunities you're exposed to. You'll get access to the most interesting and challenging projects, projects that will not only give you a lot of exposure, but will really push you to exceed your own levels and give you a strong reason to get up in the morning.

On top of this, you'll be among the top 10% highest paid people in your organization, and have influence that extends beyond your title and responsibilities. You'll gain wide recognition and be able to have a much bigger impact on your organization.

All of this will give you a new sense of confidence as you're now getting public recognition for your skills, abilities, and character. Everyone in your organization will know you as the person who can get things done. What are the benefits of this? People will trust you, there'll be less micromanagement, and you'll have a greater degree of autonomy in your company, allowing you to tackle projects in the manner you choose. Projects that will excite you and get you noticed.

Here's a (repeated) warning though: **Action is where the magic happens.** So many people read books, attend seminars, go through courses... but they don't take any action.

Why else would there always be a new fad diet every year? It's because so many people want to lose weight, but they fail to take action, always seeking that magic pill which will get them the results they desire. You know what the secret ingredient is to getting results? Actually acting on the new information.

Tony Robbins says it best:

"Knowledge is NOT power. Knowing a concept is only of POTENTIAL value to you. The execution of the knowledge you've gleaned is where your power lies."

It's really up to you. You can choose to read this book and think, "Yeah, that's pretty true," or "Yeah, I'm sure that would work," and still be in the same position where you are a year from now.

Or, after reading this book, you can get the ball rolling based upon the action steps I outline for you, and within a year you can get a new job title and have control of your career.

It's up to you.

#2 Counterintuitive Ideas

As you go through this book you're going to be exposed to some counterintuitive ideas. Some of these ideas will make you deeply uncomfortable, and that's okay.

I'm going to ask that you keep an open mind and try out some of these ideas anyway. Why?

Because currently, your mindset and actions are those of the 90% crowd, and there's no way to differentiate yourself from the rest of the masses. Plus, there are too many of you competing for a relatively small number of positions.

The only way to get extraordinary results is to behave in an extraordinary manner. Ordinary breeds ordinary, or as Jim Rohn so vividly puts it:
"Casual leads to casualties."

Learning and trying out new behaviors, such as saying "No" to new projects and focusing on your One Big Thing, will probably be uncomfortable at first. But once you get through the initial pain period, applying counterintuitive ideas of the Career Acceleration Formula to achieve 10x results... it all becomes enjoyable.

If you're doing this for the first time, how I envy you! The fun you're going to start having when you see that these new ideas work is unimaginable. You'll become eager to use them more and you're never going to look back.

#3 Unlearn In Order To Learn

Another invisible force that could be holding you back from getting the career success you want is the knowledge you already have.

You might have learned some strategies in the past that promised to get you ahead, but they may, in fact, be counterproductive because:

"It's not what we don't know that gives us trouble, it's what we know that ain't so."

Thus, in order to pave a new road to your next job title, we're going to have to destroy the old roads you've been travelling on. We need to unlearn your limiting beliefs. One example of a limiting belief you will need to unlearn and which many employees have is, "If I work harder, success is sure to come."

Working harder *does not automatically lead to success.* On the contrary, its only accomplishment is to turn you into a martyr.

Throughout this book, I'm going to take the place of your mentor. It is a mentor's responsibility to tell you *what you need to hear, not what you want to hear.* So I will do exactly that. Because just like a good mentor, I want you to achieve great success.

That is why, over the course of this book, I'll be sharing my ideas and strategies with you which will shock you, and that you won't want to hear. But I'll do it anyway, because I know that you need to know the truth in order to start getting the success you want.

#4 Ordinary Joe and Extraordinary Jennifer

The fourth thing that you can expect in this book is to learn about two people, Ordinary Joe and Extraordinary Jennifer. I'll use both these characters to help illustrate certain concepts throughout the book. Let's meet them.

Ordinary Joe

Ordinary Joe has been working at a Fortune 500 technology firm for 10 years. He works hard, always putting in extra hours when a project nears the deadline. However, no matter what he does, whether it's offering to volunteer for a project or attending networking events, his career is stagnating. Like a train unable to summon enough locomotive power to go up a hill, Joe is stuck, and it's only a matter of time before the stall in his career starts to reverse on itself and his career declines.

No matter what Joe does, his name never comes up with senior staff. He's tired of seeing his peers get promoted over him and having others question his choices and his ideas. On top of all that, Joe's self-esteem has taken a real battering from the decline in his career.

Joe views the world as a zero-sum game. This is what I call "scarcity thinking." I'll talk more about it later, but essentially Joe views the world as something he has to compete with others in. He thinks that there are limited rewards, and that he has to fight and bully his way to get the top.

Joe often applies for any jobs that come up within his firm, submitting dozens of applications a week in the hope that one of them turns out a winner, like betting on horses. This is what I call "hope marketing," and I'll share later why it doesn't work.

Extraordinary Jennifer

On the other side we have Extraordinary Jennifer. On the surface there doesn't seem to be many differences between the two. That is, until you look at their success.

Jennifer has been working in a finance firm for six years. Jennifer chooses to work smart, instead of hard. When you meet her she is quite relaxed and calm, and there are some days when she leaves the office early. Yet Jennifer has experienced rapid career advancement. She has spent 1-2 years in each job she's had before getting promoted. She is often in the top 10% of highest paid people for that career level in her company, and she never worries about the dilemma of being "out of sight, out of mind" when she takes a vacation. She knows that she's delivered enough of an impact to be on everyone's minds when she returns.

Jennifer has a high level of self-esteem and she feels a strong sense of control over her career. She has what I call "abundance thinking," she views the world as unlimited in scope and opportunity. She sees opportunities as something that she creates.

Average Joe loses when he...	Focused Jennifer wins when she...
Lives by common career advice (friends, family, Internet, career coaches)	Ignores common knowledge, applies 10x (exponential) thinking, and asks herself, "How can this be done 10 x faster?"
Works hard, not smart (too many projects, gets close to burnout)	Focuses on One Big Thing (more about that later in the book) and constantly renegotiates her priorities with her boss

Never talks about his success because he thinks that results should speak for themselves (this is driven by a limiting belief)	She delivers results AND knows how to promote her successes
Often complains about the "office politics," especially when things don't go well for him	Understands how NOT to play the office politics game, but instead masters the art and psychology of ethical influence and becomes unstoppable
Doesn't get his boss on his side, doesn't recruit mentors	Strategically builds relationships with her boss and top mentors
Doesn't leave any time for learning, is constantly firefighting	Learns and invests in herself ("The more you learn, the more you earn")
Always plans to work on his career, but allows everything else to be a priority	Puts her career development first
Is stressed out and always one step away from burnout	Is centered and knows how to stay resilient

Your strategy to achieve rapid career access will be based upon the exact step-by-step formula that I used to help me catapult my career. I went from an underpaid sales representative to becoming a Global Product Director managing a portfolio worth $5 Billion. Yes. Billions. As in, a thousand million dollars, in six short years.

I'm not promising that you'll have the exact results that I did. I am saying that it's up to you how far you go once you start applying my formula.

#5 Celebration

One thing that is important to keeping your career momentum going through the challenges and setbacks, and to keep you motivated, is to frequently celebrate your small successes.

Why am I talking about this? Because most people with an achiever mindset, including myself, suck at this. We work hard to get the results we want, and then when we get them, we immediately move on to the next goal. On the surface this might seem admirable, but in reality it means that your momentum stalls, and you don't get the success you want.

Celebrating in any way, whether it's by going for a drink or dinner with your friends or partner, or physically celebrating by dancing and jumping around is important. Why? Because frequent celebration primes your brain for success. By celebrating, you start to activate the reward circuitry in your brain, which in turn makes you look forward to achieving your future goals.

So get into the habit of frequently celebrating whenever you achieve a small milestone in the formula you're about to learn.

WHY IT'S POSSIBLE FOR YOU TO SUCCEED

When I started my own journey of career acceleration, I had a lot of things against me. I was living in a foreign country for the first time in my life. I didn't have a proper work permit. I only had enough money to last three months, after which I'd starve. I had a girlfriend who wasn't working. My accent was strong and difficult to understand (English is not my native language). I didn't have a network, coach, mentor, or a sponsor. Nada. Zilch. I didn't have the experience that was required for the role I wanted. What's more, I had to learn a new language within six months, or else I'd be let go.

These would be handicaps in any other circumstances, but because I used the strategy that you're going to learn, they ended up being completely inconsequential to my career success.

Based on my personal experience and the experience of thousands of my students and clients, I can now firmly say that you, too, can land a job promotion within the next 6-12 months without playing office politics or becoming an office martyr, staying till the lights are off and coming in before the doors are open.

In fact, most of my students have gotten promoted within much less time, in as little as 3-4 months, after applying the principles I've shown them.

Because you have picked up this book, you can already ask yourself, "Where would I like to be in my career in 6 months? 12 months?"

Before we get going and reveal the strategies, it's important to highlight who this book is for.
These strategies will not work for you if you're in a very small organization with no clear next level opportunity for you. The overall mindset and strategy behind the tactics I'll show you will get you ahead in a small organization, but you'll need some of your own creativity to make it work.

These strategies also won't work if you're not ambitious or interested in advancing your career. If you're happy with your position and paycheck and really aren't that fussed over your career, then this book isn't for you.

If you are an ambitious professional working for a medium or large-sized organization and you are failing to progress in your career after some time, then this book is for you. It doesn't matter the sector you're in, the principles you're about to learn are timeless and have worked for people in nonprofit and government, to people in finance. It doesn't matter whether your organization is a publically-traded company, or is privately held. It doesn't matter if you work in Oxfam or the Red Cross, or you're in Goldman Sachs or Google. These strategies have been proven to work for employees in over 20 different sectors and in dozens of Fortune 500 companies.

If you desire to advance your career, if you are tired of being left behind, of having your career stall and not moving, of seeing others in your organization pass you by, then this book is for you. If you wish to rapidly advance your career, kick start your own success, and are willing to put in a little bit of work to make it happen, then this book is for you.

However, there is a catch. The 6-step formula you will learn in this book works only if you are willing to implement what you learn. Action is where the magic happens. Action is what separates winners from losers. Action is what will get you out of career stagnation and straight into the 10% club. So the question is, are you ready to take the formula and implement it?

Your Safest Investment Of All

If you are willing to learn and implement the formula, great. Because if you apply what you're about to learn, you will find yourself jumping ahead everyone else.
It is common knowledge that the more you invest, the more chances of success you have. In order to gain something, you must first give something in return. That isn't just limited to financial investment. We also invest in our appearance, which we know is a critical factor to making a good impression. A favorable

impression with the right person can be priceless. It's not just simple vanity that pushes us to purchase that expensive suit, or to go to that expensive hairdresser. No, it's the knowledge that we're making an investment that can pay off in unimaginable ways.

Yet this attitude of investing for our success, which most people would agree with, doesn't seem to translate to the most important investment of all, our education.

Investing in your knowledge and your skills will offer the best ROI in not only your career but also your life. You can lose your house, your income and your savings, but you can't lose what you've learned or your *ability* to learn. These will always be of value. After all, in this turbulent period, no company can predict what skills will be critical to their organization in five years' time.

Why is this particularly important for you? Because education, your self-education, allows you to specialize, to be able to offer something to your organization that no one else can. Something that your organization doesn't have the resources to supply itself but desperately needs. This is why learning agility has become the top quality for the 21st century job market, and why your company will not only handsomely compensate you for it, but will also put you in the 10% club.

With the ever growing availability of a variety of courses online and offline, the wealth of books being written on everything you ever wanted to know, the possibility to easily get in touch with the top players in the game and make them your mentors via LinkedIn or email, it has become easier than ever to invest in your future by investing in your education. More precisely, self-education. Because, as Jim Rohn put it,

> *"Formal education will make you a living;*
> *self-education will make you a fortune."*

Just look at some the most successful individuals of today who are living proof of that:

Bill Gates' reading habits are legendary. While he was CEO of Microsoft, he would allocate one week a year, completely dedicated to reading. During this week, he would lock himself away in an office with a stack of books and other reading materials he'd been putting off during the year. No one was allowed to disturb him. No phone calls, no meetings. The only person allowed into the room was his assistant, and that was with his lunch. Despite leaving Microsoft, Bill Gates hasn't stopped doing this. You can find his book reviews and his reading list over at his blog, www.gatesnotes.com. With this reading list, he is enhancing global healthcare and eradicating extreme poverty.

Bill Gates is worth $79.2 Billion.

Elon Musk, Co-Founder of PayPal, CEO of Tesla and CEO of SpaceX, is also an avid reader. As a first grader in South Africa, he would read for 4-5 hours a day. When he started SpaceX, he literally taught himself rocket science by reading textbooks and talking to top engineers in the rocket industry for two years (his previous background was in software). The result? The other title he holds over at SpaceX, Chief Technology Officer.
Elon Musk is worth $13 Billion.

Mark Zuckerberg, Co-Founder and CEO of Facebook, started an online book club as part of his New Year's resolution called, "A Year of Books," via his personal Facebook account. He reads and makes a book recommendation every two weeks to his millions of Facebook followers.

Mark Zuckerberg is worth $35.7 Billion.

Warren Buffett says that he spends up to 80% of his time reading and thinking, "I just sit in my office and read all day." Buffett says that, through reading hundreds of pages a day, his knowledge builds up, much like compound interest.

Warren Buffett is worth $66.7 Billion.

Mark Cuban, tech entrepreneur, owner of the NBA Dallas Mavericks, and an investor on the TV Show Shark Tank, despite having never formally studied technology, software or business, credits his success to his habit of reading.

"I read every book and magazine I could. Heck, three bucks for a magazine, twenty bucks for a book. One good idea would lead to a customer or a solution, and those magazines and books paid for themselves many times over."

Mark Cuban is worth $3 Billion.

Invest in your education. You won't regret it.

Success Is A Skill And It Can Be Learned

So you may be thinking, why will the strategies of Promoted work for you? Why should you try something new when all these years you have already tried so hard and still failed to advance your career?

It's simple. Because *success is a learnable skill*.

Many people believe that success is just a matter of being lucky. They believe that the reason a person got promoted or is doing well in their life is because the stars have aligned for them and they got lucky.

Of course, chance does have a role to play in people's fortunes. But it's not chance alone. Usually when you start to assess the actions of a successful individual, you see that actually all successful people have certain traits and a set of skills in common. Success is a skill, and it *can* be learned.

The alternative is to sit down and pray that your career will advance through no effort of your own. Don't get me wrong, there's nothing wrong with hope. But when it comes to effectiveness, "Hope is just slightly below wishful thinking and just above a rain dance."

Therefore if you're not getting ahead in your career, it's because you haven't yet learned that skill. You're missing a key piece of information.

Figure 2: *Without a key piece of information, getting ahead in your career seems insurmountable, like this brick wall.*

You have the desire; you have the capability to advance in your job. So all that's missing is the knowledge of *how* to get there.

Figure 3: *But once you know that key piece of information, like this ladder, suddenly the obstacle facing you becomes easy to overcome.*

This is what Promoted is.

In this book, you'll learn a step-by-step, proven system that will get you from where you are in your career to where you want to be, in a *predictable* way. All you have to do is trust the process and follow it.

But knowledge is not enough.

Action is where the magic happens. You're going to have to put in the effort and take action on this newly acquired knowledge if you want results.

Think about it. On a scale of 1-10, how important is it for you to advance your career?

Actually take a moment to write down your number. How important is it for you to get the promotion you've been dreaming about? To have the financial security you and your family deserve? To put your kids through college? How important is it for you to get a new job title with a pay raise within 12 months? On a scale of 1-10, just how important is all that for you?

If it is an 8, 9, or 10, you are in for a treat.

WHAT'S IN STORE FOR YOU

So why should you keep reading this book? What's in it for you?

In short? I *guarantee* you this:

If you read this book and you follow the system that I've outlined, you will get promoted within 6-12 months.

On top of all this, it won't be a one off. You'll have a proven, step-by-step system that you can use over and over again to accelerate your career according to the pace you want. The only thing you'll have to worry about will be which job offer and salary level to accept. You'll have a *killer skill* that will give you an *unfair advantage* over your competition.

Stop for a moment and think about that. How powerful would it be to have a new superpower that you can use to advance your career... ANY time you want?

Furthermore, as you follow this strategy and start accelerating your career you'll make more money that you ever dreamed, allowing you to pay your mortgage with ease, never have to worry about your children's college tuition, plus, you'll be able to buy whatever luxury items you desire.

As you follow this strategy, after some early success, you'll start to have top headhunters contacting you. Imagine for a second waking up to emails and voice messages from executive headhunters offering you jobs you could only have dreamed about just a year ago.

Imagine when you get called in to negotiate the salary level of your next position, you already have two or three other job offers. You've already won the negotiation before you even entered the room because you are not needy. Instead, you are in a position of power, someone with options. And in negotiations, the side with more options wins. Instead of you going out of your way to hunt for a job promotion, others will hunt you. You'll go from lagging behind in your job, to being in demand in your industry.

The scenario I outlined above is NOT wishful thinking. I have done it, more than a few others have done it. It works, and it is a game-changer.

To put it simply, after learning my Career Acceleration Formula, your career will never be the same. In fact, I dare to say that it will change your life. As you set out on a goal to get promoted and you achieve it, possibly faster than you expected, you'll realize that *the system works*. You'll know that your career's destiny is in your hands and fully within your control. All without having to work harder or play office politics, or coming off as a used car salesmen.

What's more, as you start to learn and implement the formula, you will quickly notice an increase in your self-esteem. You will walk differently, talk differently, and be perceived differently. Your colleagues will tell you that you "look very confident lately." Confidence can be the lead domino in improving all other areas of your life. The difference in making a request hesitantly and making it assertively can dramatically alter the result. Now imagine if every request you made, from your relationships, to your career to the day-to-day negotiations in life went your way more times that it didn't. Imagine just how much of an impact that would make on your everyday life. What about the impact it would have on the bigger issues, like negotiating for car credit, or negotiating with a supplier?

Confidence is key, and it is built through action and results. By taking action, you can start a loop to continually increase your confidence.

Figure 4: *Motivation, Action, Results, Confidence Cycle*

As I've said before, action is where the magic happens. If you were intrinsically motivated to take more action in more areas of your life, imagine the effect it would have on your life. Where would you be in a year's time?

DYING SLOW VS. GROWING FAST

By reading this book and making great strides in your career, you'll start to grow and fulfill your potential. As human beings we're designed to grow. If we're not growing, we're dying. There's no middle ground.

You'll find this illustrated in the famous story about Bruce Lee taken from *The Art of Expressing The Human Body*:

"Bruce had me up to three miles a day, really at a good pace. We'd run the three miles in 21 or 22 minutes. Just under eight minutes a mile. So this morning he said to me "We're going to go five." I said, "Bruce, I can't go five. I'm a helluva lot older than you are, and I can't

*do five." He said, "When we get to three, we'll shift gears and it's only two more and you'll do it." I said, "Okay, hell, I'll go for it." So we get to three, we go into the fourth mile and I'm okay for three or four minutes, and then I really begin to give out. I'm tired, my heart's pounding, I can't go any more and so I say to him, "Bruce if I run anymore," –and we're still running - "if I run any more I'm liable to have a heart attack and die." He said, **"Then die."** It made me so mad that I went the full five miles. Afterward I went to the shower and then I wanted to talk to him about it. I said, you know, "Why did you say that?" He said, "Because you might as well be dead. Seriously, if you always put limits on what you can do, physical or anything else, it'll spread over into the rest of your life. It'll spread into your work, into your morality, into your entire being. **There are no limits. There are plateaus**, but you must not stay there; you must go beyond them. If it kills you, it kills you. A man must constantly exceed his level."*

As Bruce Lee so eloquently put it, you have to constantly exceed your level, or you're not going anywhere and you might as well be dead.

If you enter the 10% club, you will no longer stagnate, but you will thrive. You will grow and you will fulfill all your potential.

Here are some of the specific benefits you can expect once you enter the 10% club:

- **Access to the top jobs**. Jobs that are often unannounced, but are the most interesting, challenging, fun, and have high impact for the organization. These jobs are often in the high growth areas and as such, are of high importance to the company.
- **You will get extra compensation and bonuses**. You will get so much money and perks thrown at you that you'll wonder how you could have ever been content being in the 90% crowd.

- **You'll get access to the top training and executive programs,** where you will get to hang out with 10% club members from other companies and elevate each other even more. Companies want to keep investing in the 10% because they know they'll get a huge return on their investment, as the 10% take action based on what they've learned.
- **You'll get mentored by the top senior executives and VPs** in your organization. You'll not only have access to advice from living legends, but also have them personally invested in your success.
- **You won't be pressured to fit in**, on the contrary you'll be encouraged to develop your uniqueness. Your organization is looking for leaders to help them grow in these uncertain times, and it's your unique insights that will get them ahead.
- **Your job position will be immune**. Many people talk about job security, but I like to talk about job immunity. In the 10% club, your job position will be immune from turbulent market conditions. You'll have top recruiters fighting over you, your bosses loving you, and the enduring admiration of your colleagues. You'll have more job offers arriving in your Inbox than you'll know what to do with.

In short, once you've made it to the other side, once you've entered the 10%, you will **see your career in a whole new light**, and you won't want to leave. Life will never be the same again.

Over the next few chapters you'll learn about story, and the six different steps in my Career Acceleration Formula. You'll learn how to develop the correct mindset, how to increase the value you bring into the organization, and how to increase your leverage so you can get an unfair advantage over others. It took me years to learn all this, but once I did, I started getting promoted year after year. And I know if you apply this formula, you'll start getting the success you desire.

"After going through Career Acceleration Formula, I ended up getting promoted to a job role or title that didn't exist before... It was a win-win for everybody."

- Paul,
Career Acceleration Formula student

Chapter 2

MY JOURNEY TO CAREER ACCELERATION

Before I tell my story, I want to point out that the principles and strategies I'm going to share work in a wide variety of industries, in public and private settings, across all continents. In fact, what I teach has been proven to work in 23 different countries so far. I have personally lived and worked in Europe, Asia, and the US, and my students work for large Fortune 500 companies, names such as Google, Oracle, Credit Suisse, Ford, Accenture, Ralph Lauren, along with many medium-sized organizations. As long as there is a way up and you're willing to have an open mind, you're willing to take action based upon what you learn, then you're going see results in your career progression.

One more thing - if you're eager to dive into the formula, you can skip this chapter and my story. However, if you want to learn more about my personal story and what inspired me to create the formula, then I invite you to read this chapter first.

MY FIRST IMPORTANT LESSON

"I'm sorry Bozi, but it was a hard decision. After careful consideration we've decided we have to let you go..."

I didn't really hear anything after that. I was stunned. It had been a simple mistake. I didn't think it was large enough to get me fired. But I was wrong. And I paid for that mistake.

It wasn't what I failed to do with the customer that got me fired. It was the other mistakes I made. Mistakes that could have killed my career progression if I hadn't learned to fix them.

But let me back up a bit.

Straight out of University, I entered the workforce as an entry-level sales rep in the pharmaceutical industry. With my high grades and my determination to succeed, I was sure to be on the fast track to success.

However, I had limiting beliefs about sales that I wasn't even aware of, almost like invisible scripts that drive all of your decisions from the back of your mind without you being aware. I thought, at the time, that my job meant I had to be a used car salesmen, or a con man that manipulates grandmothers into parting with their pensions. I thought it was a sleazy job, and these beliefs were hurting my performance.

After a few months of not getting any results, of feeling like a loser and hating my job, I realized that there was something missing, some information that could improve my performance at work. I decided to order my first educational product outside of school. In 2003, I ordered Brian Tracy's *Psychology of Selling* and was blown away.

Let me tell you something, those CDs changed my life (yes, I still used a CD player in my car back then). Once I started listening, I became a full convert to the power of personal education and how it can affect your life. It's why over the past 12 years I've continued to spend $20,000 per year on my personal development via online courses, seminars, and masterminds around the world.

I would go out on sales calls during my typical eight-hour workday. Five of those hours were spent driving around in my car, listening to Brian Tracy talk instead of listening to the radio or music. The remaining three hours would be spent with prospective customers and existing clients. But during those five hours in the car, my brain was getting re-wired.

I was learning about the power of sales and the psychology of influence. I would listen and deeply think over the material. Then I would apply what I'd learned in my sales calls during the day.

The results were astonishing. Within three months of ordering the product, I had the top sales results among the fourteen members of the sales team. I was making more money, and I was enjoying the thrill of being successful at my job. Success was mine, and I was on top of the world.

It was during those three months that I learned three important lessons. First, personal education can change your life, if you're willing to invest in it. As we've already referred to, self-education will make you a fortune, while formal education will only make you a living. Second, I learned how to put myself in someone else's shoes, a critical lesson if you want to be successful in your career. Finally, I learned action is where the magic happens. It's only by taking action that you can truly learn something. If I'd only listened to those CDs without going on any sales calls, then I wouldn't have learned anything, and I wouldn't have gotten the results.

However, there was a problem. I was becoming way more successful than my peers, and at the same time, I didn't spend any time or energy managing my peers or my boss. That turned out to be a critical mistake.

One bright Friday afternoon I was invited to an interview with my boss, who was also the business owner. I thought I was going to be congratulated, and perhaps receive some tips on how I could improve and get ahead in my career.

But, when I walked into the office, I knew something was wrong. By the looks on the faces I saw in the room, I thought someone had died. My boss looked grim, and there was a woman there to act as a witness. Her face also looked foreboding.

I was in trouble.

"Listen Bozi, your results are very good, but you do too many things on your own. For example, we just had a complaint call from one of the customers that you manage and..." my boss began.

I knew exactly who that customer was. In my mind, the issue we had with that customer was not a major one (and it wasn't).

I became defensive. I was a blazing success right? Results should speak for themselves right? I told them as much.

"I hear you, but what about the results I've been delivering to you over the past three months? Surely that must count for something."

"Well maybe, but we have the reputation of the company to think about."

I continued being defensive, and the interview ended with a promise to talk again on Monday.

On Monday I was fired.

"I'm sorry Bozi, but after careful consideration, we've decided we have to let you go..."

Over the next week I was devastated. I was in shock. How can this be? Is this a bad dream that I am going to wake up from at some point? I felt numb, and couldn't find it within myself to feel anything. Fifteen months in and I was fired from my first job. Anger, denial, shame, depression, you name it, I went through it. Talk about damaging a young man's confidence.

I felt like a broken man. I thought I was destined for success, but now I had let myself down. I had let everyone who invested in me down. Or that's how I felt. My career was a strong part of my identity. My job wasn't just my job. My job was how I chose to walk through life. I wanted to know the "why." I knew I had to learn from this to move forward. I never, ever wanted to undergo the shame and shock of being fired again. I wanted to learn something from of this experience so it would never happen again.

It took me months to figure out why I lost my job, and it had nothing to do with the mistake I made with that one customer out of the dozens I'd served.

It was simple and yet profound. I didn't understand that *results aren't enough*. I stayed in denial for several months, saying to myself that my results are the only thing that matter, that everything else is for schmoozers. It took me years to realize that I was actually a victim of my own limiting beliefs about work and success.

Also there was something else: **No one had taught me how to navigate my career**.

No, honestly. I had gone to school my entire life. I was a good kid, I did what I was told, earned high grades, and was promised that in return for all this hard work, I would do well in life. But this was all bullshit.

Think about this, in my entire fifteen years of education, no one, not a single person, had taught me how to navigate and advance my career.

Career, relationships, parenthood. Probably the three most important areas of life. And we get no education about it.

This is why I think there are invisible forces holding us back in our career. We're simply not taught these things. I went into my first job with the naive assumption that if I were good at my job, the results would speak for themselves.

I learned a valuable lesson that day when I had to pack up my things and walk out the door: Results are not enough.

You have to learn how to ethically talk about your success, learn how to manage your boss and colleagues so you don't stir up any resentment. Those were the baby lessons I learned over the months to come.

Losing my first job was a serious setback. It was a blow to my confidence. I won't lie to you; it took me months to recover.

But when I did, I was determined to succeed. I was determined to keep moving forward in my career.

THE PROBLEM WITH OVERCOMPENSATION

After three months I got a very similar job in a different company. There's not a lot to talk about here, apart from that this is when I made the second big mistake of my career. In my previous job I'd gotten in trouble for being too results oriented, not minding to bend the rules. This time I went to the other extreme. I started spending my time trying to fit in, getting along well with others, and not rocking the boat. I was playing Mr. Nice Guy, a guy who is a smooth talker but doesn't really bring in any great results.

In less than a year I hated my job. My career wasn't going anywhere and others seemed to be doing much better than me. I started to think, *"Really? Is this what my job and career will be about?"*

In other words, my career was stagnating. I was getting left behind, feeling like a failure with each and every day and I couldn't see the light at the end of the tunnel.

During those days I would wake up, shower, put on my suit and go through the motions of getting ready. I was an automatic robot because I wouldn't allow myself to feel, otherwise I'd never get out of the house. One day, as I parked my car outside the office, this overwhelming feeling of despair took over. I had the overwhelming urge to scream, punch my steering wheel, and go anywhere else but to the hated office. I knew what would happen if I kept on going. I knew the bullshit I had to expect during my workday. I hated my job.

After some time, I'd had enough. I sent the shortest email I'd ever written in my life.

"Today, I quit my job."

I left and never looked back.

FROM A BROKE STUDENT TO MANAGING A $5 BILLION PORTFOLIO

One day, a year later, I found myself standing in the street and I couldn't believe what was before my eyes. Here I was, a Masters student living on barely $800 a month, and before me was the latest model black BMW, complete with a driver, to pick up and take me to my job interview, all courtesy of the company.

That was when I knew I was onto something with these 10% strategies.

Life was never going to be the same for me again.

But how did I get there?

After being burned out by my two jobs in sales where I literally hated my life, I knew it was time for a change. I took almost a year off to recharge and reflect. I needed a change in my career, but I didn't know how to go about it.

During this time of reflection, I stumbled across this Venn diagram that details the "career sweet spot."

Figure 5: What You're Good At / What You're Passionate About / What The Market Wants / Career Sweet Spot

I thought about that Venn diagram a lot. I took multiple personality tests to find out what my strengths were, and did a bit of introspection to figure out what I was passionate about.

During all this time, instead of working on my resume, I also started to deeply think about extraordinary ideas. What strategies could I apply to get a 5x better result in half the time?

What Archimedes lever could I apply in my own day-to-day work to get me in the top percentage of successful employees?

After some soul-searching I realized that I am passionate about marketing. Even though I didn't have money at the time, I started searching for a business school where I could get formal education in the area of marketing. I found one. It was definitely not one of the top 100 schools in the world, but I was able to get the funding and dive into the world of marketing.

While at the school, I further narrowed down the industry and environment for me, based on what I'm good at and what the world needs. I wanted to work in a Fortune 500 pharmaceutical/biotech firm in Europe. This is when I made my first 10% club vs. 90% crowd decision.

In the business course I was taking, I met someone with a parallel background to mine. Martin and I had similar goals; we both wanted to work in a Fortune 500 company, we both wanted a position in marketing. However, his approach was based on the usual advice we've all been given. He went to dozens of career fairs, shotgunning his resume to as many people as humanly possible with the hope, *the hope*, that one of the companies would bite.

What he did is the equivalent to throwing spaghetti on the wall to see what sticks. This idea just didn't sit right with me. When I asked myself what my business heroes would do in this situation, I couldn't see that method being used. I couldn't picture Brian Tracy going around passing his resume to anyone who would take it, crossing his fingers that one of them would bite and give him a call back for an interview.

This idea that shotgunning your resume alone would get you the desired job is embraced by 90% of the people. But the other 10%, the percentage of successful people who easily build their careers and design their own destiny, realized at some point that this was complete hogwash.

Aware of this, I did something risky, something radical. Something that started to put me in the 10%.

In 2005, I went online to a relatively new website called LinkedIn. It had about four million users at the time. I found the largest pharmaceutical company in the country, and then I discovered the profile of their general manager.

After some digging and guesswork to find his email address, I sent him a simple email pitch, where I introduced myself, talked about a problem the organization had, and gave a few ideas I had on how to solve it.

Read that again and notice what I did.

I didn't apply through the company's online resume portal. I didn't call up HR. In fact, I completely bypassed that department. HR is empowered to do one thing only, to say NO to you. HR doesn't have the power to approve someone who has a contrarian way of thinking. Yet this is exactly what a company needs to thrive in today's competitive market. If you want success in your career, you have to start seeing HR for what they are when it comes to staffing - the gatekeepers. There is always a way around the gatekeeper.

Such as sending a compelling pitch via email directly to the hiring manager.

Notice something else: I said I talked about the company's problems. I mentioned nothing about my desire for a job. I sent a specific targeted approach to the general manager that was sure to get his attention, as opposed to a generic mass-market approach.

And here's the thing, I didn't even have a resume!

This was a strategic play, and it paid off.

Within a day, I received a response. After some correspondence, he surprised me with this bombshell:

"I want you to interview for a role that will be open in three to four months."

I want you to think about that for a minute. Instead of spending pointless hours crafting my resume, I sent a simple email after an hour of research and was invited to interview *for a job that wasn't even open yet.*

I'd found a way to get an unfair advantage, bypass the competition, and enter the hidden job market, without a network. All by using the power of timeless psychological principles.

That's the power of thinking like the top 10%.

That takes me back to the beginning of this story. There I was, a business student, living in a cramped apartment on a tight budget, dreaming of luxuries while eating plain food, when a few days before the interview I miraculously managed to land, I am informed by the company's president's assistant that there will be a car sent to pick me up.

I couldn't believe it. No, as in I literally didn't believe it until the chauffeured black BMW showed up outside my front door on the morning of my interview.

I was a student, just some young man who had sent an email to a company, and now I was getting VIP treatment.

This was when I knew for sure that my strategies worked. This was when I knew it was time to abandon the mindset of the 90% crowd, and enter the mindset of the 10% club. This was when I knew life would never be the same again. I would never be a failure ever again.

It took six more interviews, but I got the job. I was a Junior Brand Manager, and it was my dream job. I would have the responsibility of launching a new product, every marketer's dream gig.

My first step to career fast track had begun.

I Had To Succeed

But it wasn't all rosy. There were still a few problems. In fact there were huge problems. This was one of the toughest periods of my life.

Part of my job requirement was learning a brand new language in six months. I don't know about you, but language skills aren't a great strength of mine. I had to invest 450 hours over the course of six months (on top of my daily job) to learn it. But I knew I had to, otherwise I would lose the job.

On top of the language requirement, I didn't have a proper working permit. This meant I had to apply for a working permit every six months. Fun story: If I'd gone the traditional route of the 90%, companies wouldn't have gone through the hassle of sponsoring my work permit. Yet because the general manager liked me so much, he hired lawyers to help my application.

My working permit was up for renewal twice a year. This meant I could lose the right to work every one hundred and eighty days. This created a lot of uncertainty in my life. In addition, although I was getting paid, it wasn't enough to cover the expenses of both my girlfriend and I, who at the time couldn't work. There were days where I felt like a duck, calm and serene on the outside, but paddling furiously underwater. I was anxious it was all going to fall apart.

To say things were tough would be an understatement.

But this meant one thing: *I had to succeed.* There was a lot at stake. Though I'd gotten my dream job, I still had a lot to prove. I still had to get promoted, fast, if I wanted my life to improve. Then I could get more certainty in my job.

Oh, and guess what? I was one of the only three foreigners in this organization of 600 people (it was a country subsidiary of a large pharma/biotech firm). There was no senior person to put me under their wing, no credibility to make others trust me, none of that.

Yeah. Things were tough.

I HAD to make it. I needed the money. I needed the job certainty. I needed to feed and clothe not only myself, but also my girlfriend. I couldn't just coast by with my previous success. I had to find other 10x strategies to get the financial and job security I desired.

So, how did I go about securing my success? If you remember, in my last two jobs I'd gone to two extremes, I'd gone from blindly focusing on results and neglecting everything else, to being Mr. Nice Guy who tries to fit in and talk smoothly (a.k.a, a schmoozer). I was determined to not repeat either of these mistakes.

I used these lessons to immediately start managing my boss. I started going against common thinking and recruiting top mentors.

Also, because I *HAD* to succeed, I was on the lookout for other 10x strategies from social science and psychology on how to build relationships, how to network, and the most important part of your job, how to talk about your success in an ethical manner.

Many people struggle with how to talk about their success in a way that is not sleazy, but I figured out how to in a way that is not only ethical, but effective. That is something you'll learn about in Chapter 6.

So how did I go about applying all these lessons? I went against the common mindset and, as a Junior Brand Manager, I reached out to the Head of Sales and asked him to be my mentor. A Head of Sales who led a sales force of 450 people. *Talk about _influence._*

I started to hang out with the 10% club at all times, applying the halo effect, so that people would subconsciously associate me with other fast risers in the company.

I learned how to always keep the conversation centered on my One Big Thing (more on that in Chapter 6) and how to say no to other projects and tasks. Many employees believe they have to say "Yes" to new projects or that they'll lose their job, or lose their manager's respect. This is so far from the truth, it's unbelievable. I learned how to say "No" in a way that my bosses would nod their heads enthusiastically, agreeing with my arguments.

What were the results of all this?

Within nine months, the general manager who had batted for me to get into the company nominated me for The Top 25 European Talent program, despite the fact I was fairly new to the organization.

This is just one side effect of recruiting the right mentors, something you'll learn about in Chapter 9. This is a side benefit for not just your job, but for your entire career.

The nomination brought me a tremendous amount of visibility. I was promoted to a Brand Manager, in charge of the launch of a promising new product for an entire country.

Over the next year, I continued experimenting with my strategies and refining my ideas. I ensured that my career was my priority by spending the first 10 minutes of my day on the bigger picture, and the first hour on my One Big Thing, making sure that I wasn't overwhelmed and didn't miss the forest for the trees. Soon after, I was promoted to a Brand Director role and was managing a team of people and had my own P&L (profit and loss) responsibility.

That is when I started eyeing a much larger role. I wanted to move to the company's headquarters in Switzerland and work as a European Brand Director for what was supposed to be a billion dollar brand. I knew I had to be at the top of my game, and deep down I knew that this was going to be one of the major tests for my Career Acceleration Formula. I would go to work every day, apply the formula, come back home, analyze what I could have done better, and then apply it the next day. Nine months later, I got a job offer and moved to the company's headquarters. That's when I realized I have something very powerful in my hands, something that has the potential to revolutionize a career.

Guess what happened next. After only a year and a half in my new role in a completely new country, I scored a new job promotion. It was a Global Product Director role and I now managed a $5 Billion portfolio of products. Yes. Five Billion. As in, five thousand million dollars. All by applying my formula.

As I looked back on my career, I realized that I'd done it. I was in the 10% club. I'd moved up the ranks so fast that sometimes I felt like my life was a dream. One day I sat down and tallied up my success. I'd been promoted six times in six years. I had a multiple 6-figure salary that was 15 times that of what I started out with. There were some days where I literally pinched myself to make sure that this was my life.

My career situation today is what most people would call a dream career. I do what I love, what I am good at, and what the world needs. I am surrounded with some of the most talented people on the planet, I get early access to the most interesting career opportunities, I have autonomy to do things my own way, I get extraordinary recognition for my work, and I'm invited to more VIP events than I can attend. I wake up with the thrill of success and fulfillment burning down my veins. I'm eagerly conquering challenge after challenge, and I'm one of the few people who can proudly say, "I love my job."

When I looked back on just how fast I'd gone up the ranks, I realized a few things:

Success is a learnable skill. If you aren't where you want to be, despite all your efforts, then you are simply missing some information. Information that can inform your strategy.

Advancing your career is SIMPLE if you have a proven strategy, a formula you can use over and over again. And not just any strategy, but a 10x strategy. I also realized that the 10x strategies I'd used to get in the 10% club worked *precisely because no-one else had the courage to use them*. So many people have so many limiting beliefs: they have to work hard to be successful, or if they ask their manager for help they'll be rejected and it'll affect their career. This is all plain wrong, based on limiting beliefs. Once you let these beliefs go and try out some 10x strategies, you'll start to see success in your career progression.

Investment in your personal education is an investment, NOT a cost! Winners think investment, losers think cost.

Sometimes I look back on where I was. Sometimes I wonder, what would have happened if I hadn't had bought those Brian Tracy CDs? What would have happened if I hadn't been willing to invest in my informal education and take some risks?

I wouldn't have ended up having a major Fortune 500 company give me their vote of trust and let me manage its $5 Billion portfolio, that's for sure.

Bozi Dar

Chapter 3

THE CAREER ACCELERATION FORMULA

You might be thinking after my previous story, "Well ghee, Bozi, it's all great that you got rapid success in your career, but what does that have to do with me? I don't work in the healthcare industry. Why should what you did work for me?"

That's an excellent question, and to answer it, I'm going to share a quick story.

Somewhere around the time I moved to company's headquarters to work in my European Brand Director role, many colleagues of mine started to take notice of my success. They would hear about me from other people who would describe me as someone who is very successful and knows how to advance his career fast.

Soon after, I received a lot of informal invitations for coffee meetings. After we'd sit down, the conversation usually went like this:

"Bozi I wanted to pick your brain on something. I've been in the same role for more than three years now, and I am starting to feel stuck. I tried to network, I applied for a few jobs here and there, but nothing has yet come to fruition. I am not sure where to go from here, and I'd like to ask you for career advice."

Whenever I would hear a statement like this I would respond with, "How does that feel?"

"Well you know what... it sucks. I feel like I'm dying inside. I've started to think success in this organization isn't for me. That I must be doing something wrong, or that everyone up top hates me. Of course I know this isn't true, but I just feel like something's holding me back."

"And you know this is not true because..."

"Well I've always been successful. I beat a few hundred people to land this job out of college. I've always succeeded at whatever I've set my sights on. But for the past three years it just hasn't worked out. No matter what I try, I'm not seeing results. How the hell did you get to where you are?"

I found these kinds of meetings fun, so I started mentoring people who were struggling in their careers, giving them pointers and tips based on my own formula. I didn't really know if my formula would work for them. After all, I was the only who has tried the formula until then and I was being cautious about claiming that it would yield the same results to other people.

Interestingly enough, as I was teaching them parts of my formula, I would always learn something new from these sessions. It always reminded me of a quote, *"When one person teaches, two people learn,"* and that's how I felt.

After each mentoring session, I would write down some notes based on what I'd taught. This was especially helpful when I found out what my students' sticking points where:

"So wait... I'm supposed to say **no** to new tasks and projects from my manager? Just how do I do that?" one would say.

"Wait... I hear what you're saying, but how do I remain focused on the big picture when I've got all these tasks coming into my inbox?" another would say.

I started to find ways to break down how to approach these sticky problems. Let me tell you, there were MANY of these sessions. At one point my calendar was packed full of mentoring sessions, but I didn't mind. It was fun, and I was learning about my process at the same time.

Best of all, my students started to get the same insane results I was getting. I had lots of mentees who had been stuck in the same role, at the same salary for more than five years and were now getting promoted only three months after reaching out to me! Such success stories were giving me a tremendous amount of satisfaction.

After a while I started to notice a pattern from all the notes I had taken. I have not mentioned this before, but I have a background as a semi-professional chess player, which means that I was trained, from my youth, to think strategically. I'm always looking for the quickest method to get from A to Z, taking into account various options along the way (in chess, we call that "branches"). So I started to apply my strategic mindset to the career advancement patterns I was seeing.

I took my formula and trimmed away everything that wasn't necessary, leaving only what's essential to get the career results fast. Michelangelo once famously said that every block of stone has a statue inside it, and it is the task of the sculptor to discover it. That's how I felt about the formula. I wanted to make it super simple and easy to implement, in a 1-2-3, step-by-step manner, and then offer it to the ambitious professionals who are struggling to progress their career. I knew I was on to something big.

After one and a half years in my Global Product Director role and almost a hundred career mentoring sessions, I decided to take a year off from work.

My career was going fast, I was having lots of fun and yet, I felt I needed to gain a wider perspective on life, work, cultures, and geographies. I wanted to explore more of what I had to offer to the world, and look at things from a different angle. I applied for a sabbatical and went travelling.

After exploring Southeast Asia for six months, and meeting people from all over the world, I realized that I wanted to help more people in the world who are struggling with their careers. Helping people through 1:1 mentoring sessions were very fulfilling for me and very impactful on my mentees; however, there were a limited number of these sessions that I could hold. Around that time, I stumbled upon the power of online education and the ability to use online courses to reach larger groups of professionals who want to advance their careers. I knew that was the way to go in order to put my formula in the hands of more people.

I looked back at all of my notes from my career mentoring session. After several months, I launched an online course called, Career Acceleration Formula. When I put it out to the world, the results were stunning.

It became a bestselling course in the career world and was picked up by news outlets like IvyExec and the Huffington Post. It then also attracted people from major companies such as Google, Oracle, SAP, JP Morgan, Ralph Lauren, Ford, and many other major brands. My students were telling me that they've never seen a step-by-step system that can get them promoted fast, despite the fact that they've spent tens of thousands of dollars on career coaching and various forms of additional education, such as certifications or MBA programs. But it wasn't that level of success that motivated me to write a book.

It was when I started having *career coaches* purchasing my course that I knew I was onto something. I thought of them as my competition, but it seems this wasn't the case *if they were purchasing my course.* Intrigued, I asked a few of them why they'd purchased the course.

Their answer went along the lines of, "Bozi, you probably don't realize what you have in your hands. What you teach in the formula goes against everything we taught before. After experiencing your formula and seeing the results, I see that my coaching approach and classical career development strategies are completely outdated."

When *a career coach* tells you that what they teach their clients is outdated, and they've been unable to find any other information like this, you know you're onto something. This is their field; they'd have done all the research possible, and still couldn't find anything like my course. If a career coach couldn't find any information like this, imagine the chances of a frustrated, ambitious achiever finding this information by themselves.

And it turns out they couldn't! Some of the feedback I received from my students:

"I wish I met you before, Bozi, I would have saved myself years of frustration."

"It is amazing how much value you give. I paid way more money just for resume coaching and writing last year."

"You are the mentor I never had. Thank you for being here."

"Thank you for your career course as it has led me to a new job. As well as a 40% lift of salary. This is amazing."

*"Honestly, none of the online trainings worked for me before. And yours is the only exception. If you don't mind, I will think **of you as my one and only mentor."***

It was then I realized this movement had grown far larger than just my old mentoring sessions. It had exploded to include students from dozens of major brands, and career coaches who were struggling to find material to teach their students who wanted rapid career promotion.

It wasn't just a problem I'd solved. It was a problem that my students had. And those were just the people that had stumbled upon my course. What about the people who'd never bought an online course? What about the people who didn't ever invest in their informal education? As I've said before, **9 out of 10 people in large organizations won't get promoted in the next 12 months**. This was a huge problem that was facing people in the workforce, and I knew how to solve it.

I'd solved it for myself; I'd solved it for my mentees, for my students and for career coaches. I've used what I learned teaching them and made a step-by-step, proven strategy based upon timeless principles that will get anyone the results they desire. It's the strategy you're about to learn.

And that's why this book that you are holding in your hands will work for you.

THE CAREER
ACCELERATION FORMULA

Let's talk about the formula that's going to get your career engine moving, what's behind career acceleration. I love this formula because it's downright simple, easy to follow and it includes the three elements that you'll be using throughout the book.

Career Acceleration = Mindset x Value x Leverage

Let's break it down.

Mindset

The first element is your mindset. Why is this so important?

Well remember the 10%? The top tier of people who are on the career fast track, the elevator to success, who are promoted consistently, get paid the most, and obtain access to top mentors, VIP training and all the special perks, remember them?

The number one thing that differentiates them from the rest of the 90% is that they are aware, on some level, that all human beings have two different worlds inside them. One is the visible world. This is where our actions are visible to others. The other is in the invisible world, and this is our mindset. It's made up of our thoughts, our emotions, our principles, and beliefs. They're invisible because they are inside us. No one can tell what you're thinking or what your values are just by glancing at you. Yet, this invisible world influences our actions. Our actions stem from our thoughts, like the roots of a tree they aren't visible. Yet just like a tree, the invisible world is what actually governs and controls our visible world. It is from our beliefs and our thoughts that we decide how we're going to act.

Figure 6: *Much like a tree, it's what is unseen that that controls us and makes us either thrive or fail.*

In other words, "If you want to change the visible, you must first change the invisible" as author T Harv Eker talks about in Secrets of the Millionaire Mind. This first element is what differentiates the 10% from the 90%. It's like they're running on a different operating system, software which places them on the fast track to success.

Another way of thinking about it is to go back to our tree analogy, "to change the fruits, we should first change the roots."

Value

The second element of the Career Acceleration Formula is value. In particular, your value. The level of pay you are receiving right now in your organization is in direct proportion to the value that you are bringing to the workplace.

I'll say it once again. The level of pay you are receiving right now in your organization is in direct proportion to the value that you are bringing to the workplace.

This may be a harsh way of thinking about your job, but it's actually liberating.

It's basic business; your organization hires you to do a job that will contribute towards its profits and other metrics that are important to the company. In other words, you were hired for the value that you could bring to the table. Your company doesn't care about your value as a human being, but they do care about your value in the workplace.

So why is this knowledge liberating? Because if you know this, this secret that the 10% are always aware of, then you know how to get paid more. It's that simple. In other words, if you want to get paid more, you have to increase your value to your organization.

Apart from outright theft and other immoral endeavors, this is the most effective way I know to get paid more. Want more money? Increase your value. You'll learn more about how to do this later in the book.

Leverage

This is the final part of the Career Acceleration Formula, and it's what separates this strategy from most other career strategies you can find on the market.

Have you ever heard about a lever? It's what you use to lift heavy objects with a minimal amount of force. It's the same principle found in tools ranging from your spanner to skyscraper building cranes. Archimedes famously said, "Give me a lever long enough and a fulcrum on which to place it, and I shall move the world."

Using the principles you'll discover later on in the book, you'll find out how to leverage them to multiply the value you bring. You'll find out about how to get 10 times better results in 10 times less time.

THE SIX STEPS TO THE CAREER ACCELERATION FORMULA

Without further ado, here is the 6-step proven strategy to get you promoted fast, followed by a quick overview of what you will gain from each one of them.

Mindset
Step 1: Winning Mindset

Value
Step 2: Choose Your Perfect Next Job
Step 3: Find Your One Big Thing

Leverage
Step 4: Make Your Boss Work For You
Step 5: Grow Fast Into You 2.0
Step 6: Become the Key Person of Influence

Step 1: Winning Mindset

In this step, you'll discover the three essential elements that make up the Career Acceleration Formula. You'll learn the mindsets and attitudes that will be counter-intuitive, but will get you moving forward in your career. You'll learn the typical mistakes that prevent people from entering the 10% club, and what you can do instead. I'll warn you, some of them will make you uncomfortable, but they are based on my experience, what

I've learned from other successful people, and the accomplishments of my students.

Step 2: Choose Your Perfect Next Job

The key element to success in your career is finding the perfect job to fully bring out your potential. You'll find out the three critical elements of your perfect next job, and then how to develop and narrow down the list to three to five of your ideal next jobs. You'll learn the type of job that will allow you to "be in the zone" so that success becomes effortless. You'll find out how to identify your competitive advantage. You'll learn how to validate your choice by getting external feedback so you can choose your perfect job. Career coaches usually charge thousands of dollars for this kind of information, but you won't need to pay for it. You will find all you need to know in this chapter.

Step 3: Find Your One Big Thing

Here you'll be introduced to the concept of your One Big Thing, and how important it will be in your career acceleration journey. You'll learn how to use findings in neuroscience to control what your mind and the minds of others focus on at any given moment, and how to turn that to your advantage. You'll know how to speak about your results without sounding like an arrogant show off, but in such a way that you'll have the ears and attention of your coworkers and, more importantly, your bosses.

Step 4: Make Your Boss Work For You

In this step, you're going to learn how to achieve exactly what the title says. You won't be making your boss your ally. No, you'll learn the true power of leverage by getting your boss to work for you on the progress of your career. Christopher Columbus received financing to discover an alternative passage to India, even though he wasn't a member of the aristocracy, nor did he have any navigational or sailing skills. How did he obtain the funding? By making Queen Isabella and her court work for him, thereby granting him an unfair advantage over other aspiring explorers. You'll learn what bosses really want and how you can use the principle of micro-commitments to get them closer to what you want. Getting your boss to work for you will give you the unfair advantage to leapfrog your peers in your career. It'll be uncomfortable, but it'll be worth it.

Step 5: Grow Fast Into You 2.0

In step 5, you'll be introduced to the key distinction between how the 10% think about the next job in their career and how the other 90% do, and why one of those ways is a recipe for failure (I'm sure you can guess which one). You'll learn tactics that can "outsmart" your HR department and have jobs custom designed for you. You'll also know how to overcome the "no-experience objection" that holds you back, and create undeniable proof that you're ready for your next job. You'll gain knowledge of how to overcome your fear of not being successful in your future role and you'll also find out how the 10% approach allows you to tap into the hidden job market, which, as we've mentioned before, is a wide sea of few competitors that gives you an unfair advantage in your career.

Step 6: Become The Key Person of Influence

In this final step, you'll learn the number one skill you have to master in your career no matter what your goals are. You'll learn how to stay away from office politics and instead master the art of authentic influence. You'll know how to network strategically, who exactly to meet, and what to say to get you ahead. You'll learn how to keep yourself in high demand so hiring managers and HR fight over you. This skill allowed me to not only get high visibility, but has doubled the salary of some of my students. Influence is the "killer app" of the successful and the affluent and you'll learn some ninja tactics on how to adopt it in your career.

THE BIGGEST OBSTACLES

Here's the thing, *this strategy* is going to be *unlike anything else* you've tried with your career. It's different from the usual unfounded gibberish you find in online articles or are given by career coaches, and because of this you're going to come across a few obstacles on the journey. Here are a few stumbling blocks my students have faced initially, and how to counter them.

#1 Not Willing To Try New Things

> *"In the beginner's mind there are many possibilities, but in the expert's there are few."*
>
> - Shunryu Suzuki

As I've mentioned several times already, the advice in this book differs from all the other career advice out in the market. For this reason, some of the things I suggest will make you uncomfortable; as they'll be strategies you've not thought of or acted on before.

This aversion to change, this inability to try out something new, has held a lot of students back. But this is natural. After all we're all human, we're all a collection of habits and standard behavior.

However, as I've said earlier, if you want to get the uncommon results, you have to try out uncommon ideas.

What I'll be asking you to do is to adopt a beginner's mind, a mind full of chance and opportunity when it comes to your career strategy. Look at advancing your career not as someone who has lots of experience and is an "expert" at career advancement, and therefore has a limited view, but as someone who is a beginner, a person whose mind has just been opened to the possibility of getting promoted whenever they want within 6-12 months.

The expert enters a new field with many preconceptions and as such is unwilling to try out uncommon strategies. Though the uncommon strategies tend to be the breakthroughs, he needs to reach the next level. The beginner, meanwhile, enters a new field with a mind full of possibilities, and it's the beginner who is willing to try out new things because she sees what may be. This is why it is usually the beginners in a new field who make the breakthroughs. Just ask a Swiss patent clerk who discovered Relativity in his spare time (Albert Einstein).

When I suggest some counterintuitive strategies, such as spending 10 minutes at the start of your day, before email or meeting requests, focusing on your career, and you feel yourself over-thinking and judging the action I advise you carry out, stop and try it anyway. It's easy to allow our judgments to provoke us to not take action. This is such a shame, as breakthroughs only happen from ideas that seem contrary to common sense, the same ideas that are the victims of our discrimination. Enter into this stage of your life with an open mind, a mind full of possibilities, and you will get the best results.

#2 Failing To Commit To Take Action

> *"Action is the foundational key to all success"*
> - Pablo Picasso

You're going to have to commit to taking action on the things you learn in this book, or you won't get any results. There is no way around it. There's a cognitive bias where we feel that we need to get as much information as possible before we can make a decision, a prediction, or take action. Yet nothing is further from the truth. Studies have shown that we make more accurate predictions when we only have *some* information, as opposed to an abundance of information. There is a reason they call it paralysis by analysis.

Therefore, I suggest you sit down and write a contract to yourself pledging that you will commit to the strategies of this book for a specific amount of time. Most of what I'll ask you to do will just be small changes to your day-to-day behavior, but they won't work if you don't apply them.

Based on my experience and the results of my students, I can promise you a proven system to provide a shortcut to the results you want, yet you will still have to do the work. Reading the book is not going to be enough to get you promoted. I'll repeat that: *just reading this book is not going to get you promoted*. However, if you take action based on what I teach you and commit to persevere until you get the results... then the sky's the limit!

What would it be worth to you to feel that you're fulfilling your potential? That you're finally making big forward strides in your career, and that the pace of your advancement is purely down to you and no one else?

Take your time and actually picture it.

#3 Not Setting Aside Time To Read And Apply

Another obstacle a lot of my students face is not being able to find enough time while juggling all the other tasks in their jobs to actually study and apply the principles they have to learn.

I get it...you're a busy person. There's just never enough time at work to handle all the tasks on your plate. But do you know what a successful general does on the battlefield? Sure some of them lead from the front, but the best generals also take time to gain a wider perspective. They step back to study the terrain and to see how their forces are arranged. After gaining this wider perspective, they formulate a strategy, deliver orders, and take action.

If you don't choose to set aside time for your career advancement and make it a priority, then everything else will become a priority. You'll be stuck spinning your wheels like a hamster in a cage, never moving forward, but feeling eternally busy.

You won't be achieving *your* goals, but *someone else's* goals, wasting away the precious time you have on this earth to fulfill your potential.

How will you overcome this obstacle? By setting aside a small amount of time each day to focus on your career. Choose a time and stick with it. Choose a time to read this book, and a time to create an action plan based upon the principles you'll learn.

Losers are always rushed, always busy, and never take time out for themselves. Winners smartly take a small amount of time to see the bigger picture, make plans, and act on those plans. They only react *after* they've acted on their plans.

Here is a proven method to increase your level of commitment. Be open and communicate to your spouse or partner, or to your closest friends, that you are committing to a plan for your career and that you'll need some time for it. Don't worry, it doesn't sound cheesy. After all, if you were to begin working out, you wouldn't just go to the gym and randomly lift weights. You'd find a meal and exercise plan that has proven results and you'll carry through on the plan. So communicate that you've made a plan to advance in your career, and you'll need some time to work on it. This will not only increase your level of commitment as you have now made your commitment public, but it will also provide moral support during this adventure. And you'll have more time to spend applying the principles of the book.

I'm going to talk more about this later, but I'll show you how to use a small amount of time, 10 minutes at the beginning of your work day, to spend on advancing your career. If you carry through on this, you will feel a sense of control, and you'll start making significant progress in your career compared to the other 90% of individuals who never make any plans on how to get promoted.

#4 Not Leaving Their Comfort Zone

Here's the rub.

To enter the 10% club, you're going to have to do what the 10% do. There's a reason they're in the 10%. It's because they do some really uncomfortable things. Things that scare off the average individual. But they do them because they know the risks are almost non-existent, and the results are completely worth it. They say that you can measure the success of someone by the number of uncomfortable conversations they're willing to have.

It's not all rosy, but the results are worth it. Trust me, when you are getting the letter detailing your pay raise, you'll know that all those small risks you took were worth it.

Your mind always wants to keep you in your comfort zone. I don't want to go too much into detail over the neuroscience of this, but you were hardwired by evolution to always seek comfort.

Yet it is outside your comfort zone where all the possibilities lie, and where the magic happens. That is where you will grow. And with growth comes another intangible benefit of this entire journey, having fun. When you start to see the results, you'll start to have a lot of fun.

Figure 7: *In order to grow and learn, you have to go outside of your comfort zone. But step too far and you'll enter the panic zone. The key is to stay outside your comfort zone but to not stray too far so you get overwhelmed.*

The key is to stay in the growth zone for most of the time and get used to the uncertainty that comes with this zone. This is where you will grow and fulfill your potential. Not only in your career, but also in other areas of your life.

I know you want to stay in your seemingly safe comfort zone; I know how great it feels. But you've stayed in your comfort zone all this time and you haven't gotten the results you wanted right? So why continue doing what don't work? As the great Albert Einstein said,

"The definition of insanity is doing the same thing over and over and expecting different results."

So choose today to step out of the comfortable and familiar. To grow and experience life-changing results that will propel you into the career and life you want for yourself.

#5 Not Challenging Their Beliefs

Finally, you'll find you have some limiting beliefs regarding the strategies I suggest and your career.

What is a limiting belief? It's simply an excuse your mind comes up with about why you can't do something. For example if you keep telling yourself *"I'm not great at uncomfortable conversations,"* then you're going to believe that you're not great at uncomfortable conversations.

What we tell ourselves becomes our belief. And our belief reflects in the actions we take, which, in return, designs our life. We create an operating system for ourselves that, even though it doesn't lead us to the results we want, it is what we are comfortable with. It becomes a habit and habits are hard to kick. They become who we are. It is, no doubt, uncomfortable when these habits, our belief system, are challenged. We have come to accept them as the invariable truth. However, if you take the leap of faith and start achieving some improvements, noticeable changes for the better, you will start to enjoy uncomfortable conversations because it will bring you the results you desire.

In reality, anyone capable of conversation is capable of handling uncomfortable dialogue. But many people believe they're poor at it, which becomes a self-fulfilling prophecy.

That's the danger of limiting beliefs; they become self-fulfilling prophecies. The reason you *can* do something is because you, first and foremost, *think you can*. It all starts in our minds. "If you can imagine it, you can achieve it." Because of this, it is crucial that, while reading this book, you are willing to question your assumptions and your beliefs. If you *don't think* you can get promoted in 6-12 months, then guess what? You can't. And you won't.

But if you're willing to dare, to challenge your own judgments and assumptions... then you'll be well on the road to success.

Chapter 4

A WINNING MINDSET

Welcome to the first part of the Career Acceleration Formula, as we've said before,

Career Acceleration = Mindset x Value x Leverage

Having the right mindset is the first step in getting the success you desire in your career. Most people underestimate the importance of this, but as mentioned in Chapter 3, it's the invisible world that governs our actions in the visible world.

If you want to change the fruits, you have to change the roots.

But I have to admit; I didn't realize just how great the importance of having the correct mindset was until I'd heard about the results achieved by one of my students.

Mark's story is different from most of my other students, as he wasn't looking to get promoted. He was laid off and used the Career Acceleration Formula to land a new job in another company. And he did it all by just applying ONE mindset principle that I'll talk about.

HOW THE RIGHT MINDSET CAN GET YOU OUT OF UNEMPLOYMENT

It was after he had walked out of his 14th interview that Mark knew something had to change. He had been unemployed for six months, and was unable to "close the deal" in any of the interviews he'd had for the five different companies he'd applied to.

He knew he had to up his game.

Mark graduated from college in 2011 and landed a job as a Sales Coordinator in a supply chain company shortly after. Within a year, he was able to grow into a demand planning role. He was doing well in his job and feeling content. Life was okay.

Soon, his company underwent a major restructuring process and Mark was let go, along with others.

But that's not a problem, right? When you are let go, you just find another job. Except finding a job was difficult for Mark, as it is with many people today.

Over the span of six months, Mark was a full-time athlete in the job application game. He landed interviews with five different companies, but that's where his struggle began. He just didn't know how to come across as the "number one" candidate for the job in an interview. Usually, he responded to the interviewer's questions from the gut, as opposed to applying a specific strategy for his answers.

Being a very sharp and charismatic person with a natural gift for communication, he'd always get to the final stage of the interview process, only to not "close the deal," as he'd say. During these months he naturally felt discouraged. He found the interview process to be the "elephant in the room" of work. The part that no one talks about, and no one is willing to offer support on. He felt frustrated, and felt like it was him against the world... and he was losing.

Mark realized his problem was that he didn't have a structural understanding of the interview process. He didn't know what the other side was looking for. He didn't know how to come across as the winning candidate.

"Then I came upon your course. I listened to one of your free training videos and then I decided to get enrolled in the advanced course. I felt like this is where I needed to go. I needed to spend that money to understand what's needed in the interview process." Mark told me later.

Mark felt that, even though the course was giving advice on how to get promoted internally in your organization, that the principles would be the same to get *promoted externally* in a different organization. Which is the same thing as getting a new job with a new organization.

So Mark took the leap and bought the course. He took my first module to heart, *Winning Mindset*. Mark had initially been responding to interview questions with the first thought that went through his mind. Like most candidates, he thought the job interview process was about the organization getting to know him. So his answers were naturally self-absorbed. However, after watching my first module, he went through a total transformation. He now saw that the interview process was *about how he could help the organization*. It wasn't about getting what he wanted; it was about putting himself in the hiring manager's shoes, and seeing what they need. He shifted his entire attitude from "Give me a job" to, "How can I help?"

He landed a new interview and framed himself as someone who could help the hiring manager get what they wanted by inquiring about the business strategy. Indirectly, he was actually asking, "How can *I* help you get what you want?"

Specifically out of the gate, during the interview he asked, "How can I help you maintain and exceed your business goals?" This was key, because he was able to find out the company's goals. This made a great impression, but Mark didn't stop there.

During a panel interview with several executives and the hiring manager, he specifically asked what he could do to help the company advance further, *"As your company has been growing, what are some changes that you'd like to make to help the company grow further?"* The panel was taken aback by that question. It wasn't something candidates usually asked about.

But Mark knew that by asking that, he could position himself as someone who could get the job done. He could help the business hit their goals, if he was hired.

Mark's final question put him ahead of 90% of the candidates that every company gets. He went specific.

"How will my performance be measured if I was hired? Or to put it another way, how would you measure, and what metric would you use to show that we are improving?"

Mark asked for *specific metrics* that he could be held accountable to, if he got the job. There's a lot of psychology there, but it all boils down to the first mindset you're going to learn - *value first,* or as I also like to call it, *"How can I help?"* By giving first, by framing yourself as a giver and someone who always wants to help, you make yourself stand out, and people are more likely to help you back. Reciprocation is a powerful mental trigger, as you'll learn later.

This single mindset shift was also responsible for something else. Initially Mark used to get nervous and had to deal with self-doubt before and during the interview process, as he'd been out of work for six months. This would hurt his performance during the interview. However by switching his focus from himself to the needs of the company, Mark was no longer self-absorbed. He noticed an uptick in his confidence, as he was now *solving the organization's problems*. This allowed his talent and enthusiasm to shine through in the interview. He was able to make himself stand out from a sea of candidates with just a simple mindset shift.

The result? Mark was invited to a second interview, and then received an offer with a salary 40% higher than he had expected.

Mark couldn't believe it! With one easy mindset shift, he'd gone from being jobless for six months to landing a job with a 40% raise right out of the gate. He told me that buying my advanced Career Acceleration training was one of the best investments in his life.

Oh, and guess what? His new job is in the health and lifestyle industry, something he's been passionate about ever since he was 16 years old. So now, not only is he employed and earns a salary that provides him a comfortable life, but he works in an industry that aligns with his values. He has landed his perfect job!

Now that's Career Acceleration.

"You have to commit"

When asked about his main takeaway from his experience, Mark had this to say to anyone considering upon embarking on the journey of Career Acceleration,

"You have to commit to it. If you commit to it, commit to the principles and to using those principles with any interview process... then you will see great value."

Mark's story is also a lesson that the process you're going to learn in this book is based on timeless principles that will apply to you in whatever career situation you are in. Mark bought my course, which was specifically built to help people get promoted, but he used it to get a job and secure a salary 40% above his expectations.

If you use the principles you learn, with a little bit of creativity to apply it to your own situation, you can use it to get whatever you want in your career. Not just a job promotion, but even a brand new job, or to be in charge of that superstar project you've always dreamed of.

CAREER FAST TRACK MINDSET

All right, let's get to the meat of this chapter. As we have already established, mindset is the first element of your Promotion, and it consists of eight Career Acceleration Mindset Principles. Master these and you'll have taken the first steps to getting into the coveted club of continuously successful careerists.

Mindset #1: Value First
(Or, "How Can I Help?")

Most of the time when my students come to me for tips on how to accelerate their career, they ask the wrong questions. They ask me questions like, "How can I get more money? How can I network with the right people? What questions should I ask? How can they help me?"

Yet this is precisely the wrong attitude to have in regard to your success. The entire goal, if you want success, is to give value before you get value.

This attitude taps into the power of reciprocation. Do you celebrate Christmas? Have you ever had someone unexpectedly turn up on that day with a gift, but you didn't have one to give in return? How did that feel? You felt guilty, right?

That's because reciprocating is at the heart of how we operate as human beings. Think about it, without the firm knowledge that the other person would reciprocate, trade couldn't have existed in ancient time. Or even in modern times.

But I'm not simply talking about giving on a quid pro quo basis, where you leave the other person feeling like they owe you something. I'm talking about tapping into a force of nature that will bring you all the abundance you want. It's a fact; people are more willing to help helpful people. Which café do you frequent more often? The one where the barista is distant and miserable, serving you your coffee without making eye contact, or the café where the barista smiles, asks you about your day, and offers you some tips on their daily special? Obviously the latter, because the barista is being helpful, and on a deep subconscious level you appreciate that and want to "return the favor."

People have talked about this in different ways. Zig Ziglar, the famous business and sales coach said, *"You can have everything in life you want if you will just help enough other people get what they want."*

The best way I've found to get in the mindset of giving value first is to always think in terms of *"How can I help?"* This is exactly the simple change Mark made that landed him a job with a 40% raise after repeatedly failing to get a job for six months.

When you meet other people in the workplace, always be thinking, "How can I help?" When you meet your mentors, convey the attitude of, "How can I help?" When you meet your manager, ask, "How can I help?" When you meet your customer, what should you convey? You got it; it should be, "How can I help?"

Have these words playing on loop inside your mind during all your interactions, and you will start to change your approach from being a taker to being a giver. And you'll start to receive a lot more in your career as a result. The opportunities that will start to open up simply because people perceive you as a helpful person, will amaze you.

Mindset 2: I Am The Product

This is a difficult mindset for people to understand. When we perceive ourselves, we perceive ourselves as a human being. We perceive our character, our stories, our dreams, and our fears. Yet your organization doesn't see you that way. Your organization sees you through the output of your work. They value the outcomes that you produce, not the time you spend on the work. In other words, you are a product.

And that is a good thing. Once we adopt this mindset, once we start to see ourselves as the product, as something that can produce results, and that we can invest in to improve its quality... we can start to see ourselves from our manager's perspective.

Imagine for a second that you are the owner of your organization. Your number one priority is making the company turn a profit. Without profit, your business will not exist. Simple as that. So when you hire someone, there's only one question running through your mind, *"How will this person deliver to my bottom line? Is she going to save me money? Make me more money? Save me time? Improve our efficiency?"*

In the same way, if you are a promising candidate, then the company will invest money into you and expect a return, just as we all do with the products we buy. We invest money in them because we expect a certain result.

If you start to view yourself as the product, that the output and outcome of your work is important to the organization, and that investing in yourself will improve the outcome you deliver to the organization, then you are another step closer to mastering the mindset required to succeed.

So just remember, you are the product, so strive to be a premium one!

Mindset 3: I Work Smart, Not Hard

Have you ever seen a hamster running and spinning the wheel in its cage? It's a cute image, but it's also a reminder about something. To the hamster, it feels like it's working hard, like it's running somewhere, but actually it's staying in the exact same place. It's not making any progress, despite how fast it's running. It's where the phrase "spinning your wheels" comes from, and it is precisely what you are doing when you are striving to work harder to get promoted.

Most people assume that is what is required. But career acceleration isn't about working hard. It's about working smart. It's about making real progress, not just spinning your wheels.

Let's look back at Ordinary Joe I introduced in the first chapter. Joe is a hard worker, yet for all the long hours he puts in, his career is stagnating. I used to wonder why people would work so hard, investing their time into areas that are low leverage, and now I understand why.

Many people feel like they need to control the outcome. They feel powerless in their career, and they want to exert a sense of control. There's nothing wrong with that, but the problem is the way they go about it. They seek to gain the approval and validation of their peers, and they feel that they'll get this by slaving away. If people notice how hard they work, then people will become aware of how amazing they are, and then all the perks and bonuses and promotions will just come their way.

Of course this is not the case. It never has been, and never will be. Working hard will not get what you want. I'll repeat that **working hard will not get you what you want**. Working smart will get you the results you desire.

Another reason to not do the hard yards is the fact that you're simply not designed to do that. You're not a machine; you're a human being. We are designed to work and then recover, have fun, and rest. A study by the Draugiem Group found that the most productive people didn't work for eight hours a day, but worked less and took constant breaks. Jim Loehr and Tony Schwartz discovered after working for 30 years with the world's top athletes that, *"Life is a series of sprints, not a marathon."* So is your career.

Additionally, all the research in positive psychology in the past 20 years is pointing in one direction, happiness is the new productivity. If you're happier, you'll be more productive and useful to your organization. I picked up this lesson from Vishen Lakhiani, founder and owner of Mindvalley. And he knows what he's talking about, Mindvalley has repeatedly won accolades such as *List of Most Democratic Workplaces* by WorldBlu, and a *Great Place to Work®* certified company, putting it in the league of companies like Zappos, Google, and Cisco.

Work smart, not hard. How to do that? Wait until Chapter 6 when we introduce you to your One Big Thing.

Mindset 4: Career Success Is In My Hands (Or, "I Am In Charge And Can Control It")

It continues to amaze me, that even extremely smart people, expect their manager or HR team to provide them with a specific career plan. Heads up, as this news might shock you... it won't be. Your organization isn't your parents, they aren't going to take care of you and guide you on how to advance in your career. This mindset stems from our childhood. Our parents took care of us and directed us. Then after our parents, it was our school that did that for us. After our school, it was our college. While this thinking served us well during those years, it is completely useless in our career.

It's also a classic example of living in what I call "victim mode," a symptom of the 90%. When you're in "victim mode," you abdicate responsibility and blame anyone you can for your situation. You blame your education, your genetics, or the economy for why you aren't being promoted. People in "victim mode" spend the whole time complaining and finding reasons to support their story. This creates a self-fulfilling prophecy. They're stuck because they've weaved a story to themselves about why they're stuck. They're trapped by their story, and don't have any reason to step outside their comfort zone and find the *real* reasons why they aren't getting what they want. Why is it uncomfortable? Because they have to accept responsibility and realize they're in charge of their career. This is scary, but it's also an empowering, liberating thought.

It's empowering to know you're in charge of your destiny. This is a profound mindset shift, and it's one of the first ones I require my students to make. From being a victim to being the hero of their own story.

This means the truth is simple: No one cares more about your job and your career than you. If you want to enter the 10% club and get on the career fast track, you have to be willing to seize the controls and steer your destiny. No one else will.

The good news is that it is completely in your hands. Maybe you don't want to make VP. Maybe you want to run an autonomous division. Whatever the case, decide what you want and start steering your career in that direction.

This is another liberating thought. No longer is it up to your organization about where you go. Your path is up to you and only you. If you embrace this, you can truly go far in your career.

You must realize you have more control over your career than you think. We'll talk about this in more depth in Chapters 7, 8 and 9 about how you can control where you go with the level of influence you have.

Just remember that you get to decide where your career goes, not anyone else.

Mindset 5: Success Patterns Are Learnable

Almost a century ago, Napoleon Hill was inspired by an idea from his mentor, Andrew Carnegie. At the time, Andrew Carnegie was one of the wealthiest men on earth, with an estimated net worth of $372 Billion in today's money. Having pulled himself up by his bootstraps, he wanted to give back to the world. In addition to his philanthropic endeavors in which he gave away $13.2 Billion to charities and universities around the world, he wanted others to emulate his success. He shared this idea with Napoleon Hill, who took it to heart. He traveled around the United States, interviewed the most successful people at the time, and wrote and published his famous book, *Think and Grow Rich*, where he literally shared the blueprint of success. Ever since, countless readers have gone on to use the strategies shared to gain the success they want.

The fact of the matter is, if someone else has done it, then you can do it. Of course, there are some natural born geniuses who are inimitable and success for such people is a given. But those people are a one-in-a-million and they shouldn't be your concern Success patterns are learnable. All you have to do is emulate their success.

And remember this, every master was once a disaster.

Michael Jordan, yes THE Michael Jordan, was not allowed to play in his high school's basketball team because he "didn't have enough talent." We all know how that story ended and what Michael Jordan went on to become.

Throughout history we've known this. Before the modern university system, there was a traditional process by which society taught the next generation how to be successful. They were called apprenticeships. Apprenticeships were important because not only would the apprentice learn the skill required for the craft, but they would also pick up the other skills for success; how to deliver a quality product, how to please the client, how to build a reputation. These skills weren't formally taught, but would be naturally picked up by the apprentice as he worked with the master, allowing him to be successful in his chosen field when he set out as a journeyman.

Yet this is something we've lost in the modern education system. We focus on teaching the hard skills and knowledge required for the workplace, but not the soft skills. The soft skills that are required for success, such as having the right mindset, delivering value to others, and building influence.

Success is a learnable skill, and you're literally holding the book on how to learn to be successful in your career.

So don't be discouraged by where you are in your career. Because it doesn't matter where you are, it matters where you're going.

Mindset 6: The Best Jobs Aren't Advertised; They're Created For The Best People

The best jobs in the economy are not advertised. No, they are created for the best people. This is the hidden job market.

Let's go back again to Ordinary Joe. This is what he does when he wants a promotion... he waits for a job opening in his company or in another company and then applies for it. He then hopes that he'll get invited for an interview, without doing any work up front to secure that outcome. This is what I call "hope marketing."

Now let's look at Extraordinary Jennifer. She goes about getting a promotion in a different manner. She decides she wants to work in the high growth part of the organization. She does what I call "informational interviewing" and creates demand for herself, while building her network. By the time she goes for the interview, it's mainly a formality required by HR; she's already got the job, as it was created for her.

This is a more powerful strategy to consider when going after your desired job.

The best jobs aren't out there to be looked at; they're created by the organization for the best people. It's not hard to enter that 10% of employees who are always in demand.

Mindset 7: The Compound Effect Is The Most Powerful Force In The Universe

> *"The most powerful force in the universe is Compound Interest"*
> - Albert Einstein

Which would you rather have, $3 Million in cash at this very moment, or a single penny that doubles in value every day for 31 days?

Well maybe you'll want the $3 Million, after all I'm sure that amount of money would solve a lot of financial problems. But let's look at what happens to the penny.

On day 2, you'll have two pennies. On day 5, you'll have 16 cents. On day 10, you'll have $5.12. But this is where it gets interesting. Five days later you'll have $163.84. On day 20 ,you'll have $5,242.88. And 10 days after that you'll have **$5,368,709.12.**

If you're willing to wait and let compound interest take care of the results, you'll have over $5 Million in 30 days.

This is why the compound effect is one of the most powerful principles in the world. Banks understand it and that's why they strive to charge compound interest as opposed to simple interest on their loans. Simple interest would be the bank charging 5% every year on the principal amount of money. So if you borrowed $1,000, they'd charge you $50 every year. However compound interest is 5% of interest applied to the new sum every year, causing a result similar to the penny doubling scenario above.

But the compound effect is not just limited to financial matters. You can find it in other areas of life. For example, let's look at people who go to the gym. Many people apply for an annual gym membership after setting a New Year's Resolution, go to the gym every day for 30 days and then quit. They gain the weight they'd lost, and are back at square one.

However, other people go to the gym twice a week, but stick with it over the entire year. This small action applied consistently means they gain significant results over time. That action of going to the gym twice a week compounds to give them a spectacular new body by the end of the year.

Success really is nothing more than a few simple *disciplines*, practiced _every_ day.

When we apply this compound effect to your career acceleration, it means dramatic results won't happen overnight. You'll take a small action of focusing on your career for 10 minutes every morning, review the roadmap, and this habit will pay off exponentially in the long term.

If we choose to not seek the instant payoff of the $3 Million, but instead focus on the small action of doubling our penny every day, we can get over $5 Million in 30 days. We just have to be willing to *delay gratification*. You can and will enter the 10% club, but it won't happen overnight. However, I assure you that if you dedicate the first 10 minutes of your day towards your career, you'll see significant results in 6-12 months.

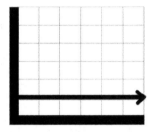 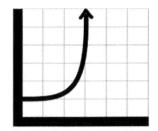

LINEAR EFFECT. NO CHANGE. COMPOUND EFFECT. STARTS OFF FLAT,
THEN TAKES OFF DRAMATICALLY.

Figure 8 TEXT A: Linear Effect. No change. TEXT B: Compound Effect.
Starts off flat, then increases dramatically.

Mindset #8: Having A Great Career Is Fun.

Here's a secret that those in the 10% club know. Having a great career is fun. In fact,

> *"Fun is the most underestimated ingredient of success."*
> - Richard Branson.

It's the Ordinary Joes who believe that they have to be downright serious about their work, that fun is only for the evening and weekends. Yet, the Extraordinary Jennifers, on the other hand, bring all they have, their serious side *and* their playful side into their work, because they know that having fun plays a pivotal role in their success.

I'm really grateful for the opportunities I've had in my career, the chances to have had a lot of fun, to meet a lot of impressive people, take amazing courses in places like Berkeley, be acquainted with extraordinary mentors like the CEO and founder of Nespresso, live in three different countries, meet awe-inspiring athletes like Ueli Steck, the fastest mountain climber in the world, and many, many other things.

There is so much fun to be had throughout your career, if you allow yourself to enter the 10% club.

And the catch? To enter the top achievers club, you have to know how to enjoy yourself in your career. Listen to Richard Branson. Go after the activities that are fun for you and your career will accelerate to the levels that you can't even imagine.

HOW TO ADOPT THE MINDSET OF THE 10% CLUB

So, there they are. These are the eight Winning Mindset Principles for your career acceleration. I don't expect you to adopt these instantly; some of them are very counter-intuitive and differ greatly from your thinking over the past few years. Therefore, don't expect to change your mindset overnight. Besides, we will be coming back to these principles throughout the book, and you'll have the opportunity to internalize them as you read on. So not to worry.

In order to adopt the new mindset principles, you will, of course, have to take some steps to adopt them. Sitting there and passively reading will accomplish nothing. As I've said, this book will be very action oriented for good reason. I've repeated it several times already because it's something I've noticed in my success, and in the success of others, *action is where the magic happens*. You're not going to get anything out of this book without acting on what you learn here. To get you started, here are the two things you ought to do right away.

Block Out 10 Minutes On Your Calendar

The first thing you'll need to do is to go to your calendar and block out the first 10 minutes of your workday to focus on your career. You can label it, "My Career" or "Career Acceleration." *Before you do anything else* at work, such as answer email or attend meetings, you'll spend these 10 minutes to focus on the bigger picture in your career.

Choose 3 Mindsets And
Put Them Somewhere Visible

Now, here's how you can get your subconscious mind to start internalizing the mindset you need for your career acceleration.

Choose and write down three of the Winning Mindset Principles that you want to adopt. For example, let's say you want to adopt the mindset principles Work Smart, Not Hard, or Give Value First, and I Am The Product. Find a piece of paper and write them down.

Then place this list somewhere visible where you'll constantly see it. Maybe you'll place it on your bathroom mirror, or on your wall at work. I know some people who've placed it inside their wallet, as they know they'll see it every day.

Figure 9: *Use daily affirmation to solidify your attitude*

Before we go any further, I'm going to ask you to stop reading now and carry out these actions. I will repeat it once more, and over and over again, until you have adopted this attitude: You won't make any progress towards your dream career if you don't take any action.

To sum up what action is required of you right now:

- Block out the first 10 minutes of your workday to work on your career in your calendar.
- Write down three mindsets that you want to focus on and place them somewhere visible.

Finally, once you've completed these actions, take time out to celebrate. Celebrating will not only prime your brain for success, it's something you deserve since you've taken the first few steps to becoming extraordinary!

To Summarize:

- Mindset is one of the foundational differences between the 10% club and the 90% crowd, and is critical to their success.
- There are eight mindsets required for the Career Acceleration Formula.
- In your calendar, set aside 10 minutes at the beginning of your work day and dedicate it to your career acceleration.
- Choose three mindsets you want to adopt, write them down, and leave them somewhere where you'll see them daily.

Chapter 5

CHOOSING YOUR PERFECT JOB TITLE

Remember our formula:

Career Acceleration = Mindset x Value x Leverage

In the last chapter, you learned about the mindset of top performers. Now you're going to learn how to raise the value you bring to the workplace by choosing the perfect job title. This job title will maximize your abilities and deliver tangible results to your organization's bottom line.

As I've said before, it's only by giving others what they want, that you can get the success you desire. By choosing your perfect job title, you'll begin laying the foundations of your career acceleration.

But before we get on with it…

As a result of the last chapter, you should have completed two actions by now: blocking out the first 10 minutes of your work day for your career, and writing down three of the mindsets that you want and putting them in a visible place.

If you haven't completed these action steps, I heavily recommend you go back to chapter 4 and do so now, because everything in this book is connected. Each chapter builds on the previous one, and each recommended action you take is a step that brings you closer to your career goal. One thing is for sure, you won't get any results if you don't take action.

So do it now!

If you have, then it's time to reveal to you the second element of your Promotion.

One thing I'd like to clarify is that this chapter is called, *Choose Your Perfect Job Title*, not *Find Your Next Job,* and there is a reason for this. Most people in the 90% crowd, when they're thinking about their next job, start going to online job boards, LinkedIn or search around the web for job titles that are applicable to them. But the biggest change in your career acceleration actually happens once YOU make a decision on what your next *job title* will be.

What's more, this new job title has to be *perfect* for you. Why? Because having a perfect career involves having a successive series of perfect jobs.

Perfect Career = Perfect Job 1 → Perfect Job 2 → Perfect Job 3…

Once you choose your perfect next job title, your career acceleration will start to materialize before your very eyes, as Paul found out.

HOW PAUL SNAGGED
HIS PERFECT JOB TITLE

Two months after purchasing my advanced online career course, Career Acceleration Formula, Paul landed the promotion he'd set his eyes on.

Paul was one of my early students. He has an undergrad, an MBA, and at the time he was working in software sales in a cloud software company in Colorado.

Except that Paul had been stuck in this role for three years.

The last year had been agony for Paul. He had already gotten the idea of progressing to a new role from his manager a year before he bought my course. He went through the traditional job promotion process. But this was where his frustrations began.

Paul wanted to advance in his company; it was time for a new challenge, and it was time for him to get recognition from the company for the time he'd invested with them.

However, there wasn't a clear path to follow from where he was to where he wanted to go in the organization. Paul didn't have a clear strategy on how to advance. He didn't want his promotion to be a result of pestering or pressuring his organization and colleagues. Instead, he wanted his promotion to be a result of the company's recognition.

When I asked Paul how this affected him emotionally, I was a bit nervous, as most men are hesitant about talking about their feelings, but Paul was candid:

"It was an ultimate frustration. I had invested a good amount of effort and time into my company, and I really wanted to leverage that and take it to the next level, but I didn't know how."

Even if Paul's company could better use his skills and strengths to their advantage, they didn't know how. There didn't seem to be a clear and open position for Paul to grow into. Finally, he admitted,"*I knew that things weren't just going to happen on their own.*"

This was when Paul came across my free training webinar.

After identifying with the pain points I talked about in my webinar, Paul purchased my course in March 2015; an investment he'll later say was "pennies on the dollar."

The thing you need to know about Paul is he's an achiever. Once he sets his mind on a goal, he runs after it, a trait that's lent well to his career in sales.

He started working through my course day and night, excited to take each step on his road to success. But the real game changer for Paul was when I suggested he should identify his natural advantages by taking a strength finder test.

When he completed the test and discovered what his natural advantages were, Paul said he felt like he'd gotten slapped across the face! He became aware that his current role wasn't using his natural talents, which finally answered the deep nagging feeling he'd had about why he wasn't happy with his job title.

Once Paul identified his strengths, he started to connect and interview as many people as possible to find a job title that'd be perfect for him. This is what I call External Validation, a third step of the three-part process of finding your perfect job, which I'll talk about later. It's a very powerful process that often saves years, if done right. These meetings helped Paul validate his next job title; it was perfect and it leveraged his strengths. As a result of these meetings, he grew more assured of his choice for the next role he wanted. Confidence can be a powerful driving force because when you know you're on the right track, you'll be more motivated to work on your career. Also, of course, increased motivation means you take action, get results, and gain even more confidence. Remember that powerful cycle that we introduced in Chapter 1, this process can add fuel to your overall happiness.

Figure 10: Motivation, Action, Results, Confidence Cycle

Creating a clear vision of the perfect next job he wanted, Paul looked at his organization and asked himself the following questions, *"Where are the gaps? What can I bring to the table that my organization is missing? How can I find the sweet spot between my strengths and my organization's unsolved problems?"*

Paul also had a conversation with his manager about his career plan. This conversation was key, because as Paul says,

"Now there's a dialogue. Now there is a discussion. Now there is a game plan and there are commitments about what it would look like."

Both parties were now on the same page when it came to Paul's career.

This is a complete opposite to the lack of clarity and planning that Paul had prior to discovering my Career Acceleration Formula course.

How The 10% Negotiate

After Paul put together his Career Development Plan and shared it with his manager and his team, it seemed all was golden. Paul finally had a clear path for his career and how to advance. Except there was one snag.

"Me and my manager had a good vision for the future, but the timeframe wasn't really the timeframe that I wanted."

His manager was thinking and talking in terms of *years* rather than *months*. Paul was looking to advance fast, and wasn't prepared to wait that long for his next role.

What Paul did next is what now sets him apart from the 90% crowd. Most workers would accept the timeframe the manager gave them. They'd start jumping through the hoops thinking that's the only way to get promoted. But the 10% understand that this is a false obstacle. There are other ways to get the results you want in the time frame you determine.

Paul started actively looking outside of the organization for his perfect role. His thinking was, if he wasn't a good fit for his company, and since he already knew his strengths, it made sense to look elsewhere where he could continue. He searched for other roles and networked with individuals in organizations other than his.

Finding greener pastures, Paul returned to his team and approached the subject again, but this time to explain that it might make more sense for him to go elsewhere.

All of a sudden, Paul turned the tables around. From the organization's point of view, here was a valuable employee who wanted to advance, but was ready to leave in order to maximize his potential.

There's a saying in negotiation that whoever is willing to walk away from the table wins. Paul was willing to walk away and this triggered a powerful influence factor inside his organization that is often called "the scarcity effect." This means that when something becomes scarce, we tend to pay more attention to it. All of a sudden, the timeframe for his career advancement was accelerated.

Paul admits that taking this sort of action was a little outside of his comfort zone, and required a bit of push and pull between him and his team, but as he explains,

"In the end, I achieved my result of going from a sales role (account manager) to a Director role and having a couple of folks reporting to me, and getting my own office."

This promotion happened on May 1st, two months after he'd purchased my course, and he was able to envision this sequence of events unfolding.

It is worth adding that Paul's new role also came with a hefty salary increase, which is what led him to say his investment in my course was "pennies on the dollar," something I love to hear from my students (as they typically add $10,000 - $30,000 to their yearly salary after they go through the course if, most importantly, they implement what they learn).

Paul's story is dramatic because his career was stalling until he identified his strengths. Once he did, he was able to start looking for his perfect job title, one that was in the sweet spot between his natural skillset and the organization's problems. Once he identified it, he was able to use the other strategies in this book to land his promotion.

Your strengths are just one of the three critical elements of your next perfect job title. Once Paul had that and had the confidence to chase the title, he knew where to look and how to create the opportunity for this job title. If he had stayed in the 90% crowd and tried to get his next job title without a clear strategy, he probably wouldn't have been promoted within two months.

Now you now know the importance of choosing the perfect next job title. But how do you go about choosing it?

THE THREE ELEMENTS OF YOUR PERFECT JOB TITLE

Let's return to Ordinary Joe and Extraordinary Jennifer and how they go about choosing the next job title in their career.

Ordinary Joe doesn't choose his perfect job. Instead, he frequently checks in with job search websites, looking for what he *imagines* or *hopes* is his next dream job. Each job description he comes across sounds great, as the grass is always greener. Except that this is never the case.

Ordinary Joe changes employment hoping things will be better, yet he always ends up back at square one. He quickly becomes frustrated with his job, and because he switches to a new company, he has to build his network all over again. Dissatisfied and alone, Ordinary Joe soon becomes discontented in his new job... leading him to repeat the search for a brighter future in his career all over again. Joe is what I call an **Opportunistic Careerist.**

How does Extraordinary Jennifer go about finding her next job? First, before she does anything else, she gains clarity on three things:

- The right environment for her
- Her strengths
- Her competitive advantage

Second, after gaining these insights, she takes a long hard look at her career. She asks herself, *"What kind of job would be ideal in both the short term and long term? What job would be the best fit for me based on my understanding of my personal strengths and my needs, defined above?"*

Third, after Extraordinary Jennifer has nailed down the perfect job title, she builds the skills and the influence in the organization required to get this job title, putting herself on the career fast track. In other words, SHE drives clarity, SHE decides what she wants next in her career, and SHE communicates it to her management. That's what I call a **Strategic Careerist.**

This is what Paul did. It was only after he had identified his strengths and defined his perfect job title that he was able to start using his influence to get that job title.

Remember how he was able to get promoted in just two months by letting his team know it might make more sense for him to leave? How did this work?

Well, think about how HR perceives people like Paul and Extraordinary Jennifer. Every now and then upper management asks HR, *"Give me an update. Who are our top talents? Who are our best assets when it comes to people?"* Based upon Jennifer and Paul's clarity of vision and their recent career advancements, their names come up in conversation. Upper management then asks HR the next critical question, *"Great, so what are you doing in order to develop and keep them?"*

This is where all the bonuses and perks come in. HR does everything humanly possible to retain the Jennifers and the Pauls and show them that they are a valued asset in the organization. They give them access to the best mentors, the top training courses, salary raises, and extra compensation. If their organization has access to it, they'll literally throw it at them. Whatever it takes to keep them.

Why? Because they are an investment. These employees are an asset that upper management and HR are certain will give a great return. Why? Because they've demonstrated their worth.

As a result, HR and upper management help them to move quickly from one job to another, as they want to develop Jennifer and Paul's capabilities further, and receive a faster and bigger return on the organization's investment. They want to give them extra responsibilities, so that they can learn and grow.

This is dramatically different from Ordinary Joe and the 90% crowd. Ordinary Joe gets left behind, and is rewarded with a minimal 2% raise each year, in order to give him an illusion of progress, enough not to be entirely dissatisfied but definitely not on the career fast track.

So what are the three critical elements of your perfect next job? What can you start doing in order to gain clarity on your perfect job title so you can start developing the leverage to get there?

It's simple, they are:

- Playing the right game
- Knowing your strengths
- Knowing your competitive advantage

Get Into The Right Game

> *"The general who wins the battle makes many calculations in his temple before the battle is fought. The general who loses makes but few calculations beforehand."*
>
> - Sun Tzu, The Art of War

The first critical element of your perfect job title is getting into the right game. What do I mean by this?

In the quote above from *The Art of War*, a treatise over 2500 years old, Sun Tzu was referring to the fact that the greatest generals have already won the battle before it has even started. How? They have studied the terrain, the mindset of the enemy, their political will, their strengths and weaknesses. They have assessed their own strengths and weaknesses, and thus formulated a battle plan that is guaranteed to succeed.

They can essentially guarantee victory before the battle is ever fought. How is that? By choosing the correct battle to fight.

And that's what I mean by choosing the right game in your perfect job title. The "right game" is the job environment, the department, the unit, the market, the business branch where your chances of succeeding are at their highest.

In the movie *Rounders,* there is a great example of the right game. The movie follows professional poker player Mike McDermott, and there is a scene where he first scans all the tables in the room before deciding on one at which to play. Once he's at that table, he looks at the competition. If he can't spot the sucker in the first half hour, he realizes he must be the sucker, and cuts his losses. In poker, choosing the right game is choosing the right table, the table where your odds of outplaying the competition are at the highest.

This is how you get the unfair advantage needed to advance beyond your competition in the job marketplace.

In my experience, choosing the right game is the most overlooked, most underutilized, and the most powerful of all the three elements of your perfect job. It can be the decision that can accelerate your career beyond your wildest dreams.

So what is the right game? Well, there are two components when it comes to your organization. The first is the department, or unit in the organization that offers you the opportunity to be **highly visible** to upper management or to the customers. It's the department that has the potential to draw lots of attention.

The second component is the area of your organization where all the **big budgets** go. There's a maxim in detective police work, and that's to follow the money. If you follow the money, you'll often find out who had the motive to commit the crime. Now, I'm not suggesting you become a criminal, but I am suggesting you use some strategic insight and look for where the money is going in your organization.

Big budgets are incredibly important because if you have a large sum of money at your disposal, you have the power and freedom to basically do what you want. It's the equivalent of turning up to a knife fight with a rocket launcher. Often, the key to accomplishing the remarkable result required in that department is by coordinating this huge budget with the correct external talent or organization that can help you get to your goal.

Because of these components, I advise my students to look for departments or units that are in one of two situations:

The Turnaround Situation: Here this part of the organization has a lot of potential, but is underperforming for reasons the organization hasn't identified yet.

The High Growth Unit: Here the unit or department is growing and is on a trajectory for further growth. There is potential for this department to become the jewel in the crown for the organization.

Why these two? Because both of these situations will offer clear visibility to upper management, as they're always at the top of their agenda. Additionally, these units are where the money goes.

I'll give a personal example, one where I actually stumbled upon this idea. I didn't understand just how powerful choosing the right game could be to my career. This was when I was given the opportunity to be promoted to a Brand Director, and a new Head of Marketing was hired. Now this guy had a problem, he was new and he needed to know where to allocate talent in order to deliver the greatest results.

He invited me to a meeting one day and gave me the chance to share my opinion on which of the three products I would like to work on. Which product would I be happy to take over? There were no promises, but what I said would be taken into consideration.

If I could turn back time, I would have asked him two questions before I made a decision. I would have first asked, *"Which of the three products is the most important for the company's **growth** in the future?"* And then I would have asked, *"Does any of the three products need a **turn-around**? Is there one that needs to go from zero to hero?"*

Like I said, I didn't know to ask those questions at the time. Instead I fumbled my way through the meeting, and I struck gold by getting the product that was important to the company's growth. In other words, I got lucky.

So before you move further into how to accelerate your career, look at getting into the right game first, because it can make all the difference in your career.

I've created a special worksheet that will help you identify the right department for your perfect job title here: www.career10x.com/bonuses. Visit the link to get it for free.

Discover Your Strengths Or Suffer The Pain Of Frustration

> *"Everybody is a genius. But if you judge a fish by its ability to climb a tree, it will live its whole life believing that it is stupid."*
>
> - Albert Einstein

Discovering and uncovering your strengths is the second critical aspect of your perfect job title. But what do I mean by your strengths? Is it your character? Is it your skill set? Is it your personality?

It's a murky question that can quickly get confusing without precise definitions.

I like to think about strengths when it comes to your career in this manner:

Your strengths are innate abilities and talents that come naturally to you. When you engage in a task that uses them, you perform your best work.

There are three symptoms of what it's like to be using your innate strengths in the workplace.

First, before you engage in such a task, you get excited. You literally can't wait to begin. You're bursting with ideas on what the outcome of the task will be.

Second, during the task, you get absorbed by the work. Mihaly Csikszentmihalyi calls this state *Flow*.

Here's one definition of flow: *"Flow is completely focused motivation. It is a single-minded immersion and represents perhaps the ultimate experience in harnessing the emotions in the service of performing and learning. In flow, the emotions are not just contained and channeled, but positive, energized, and aligned with the task at hand. The hallmark of flow is a feeling of spontaneous joy, even rapture, while performing a task, although flow is also described as a deep focus on nothing but the activity – not even oneself or one's emotions."*

When you're in flow you lose track of time, the work is almost doing itself. It's a state of perfect decision-making. The writer who writes for hours is in flow, the salesman who is closing sale after sale is in flow, the stand-up comedian who is successfully improvising on stage, coming up with joke after joke, is in flow. Watch a child playing and you'll understand flow.

Third, after you've finished the task where your strengths shine, you feel even more energetic. You don't feel worn out, instead you feel revitalized, like you just drank shot of espresso and stepped outside for fresh air.

If a task is hitting all three of your criteria, then you're in a position that's using and leveraging your strengths.

For example, let's say public speaking and communication is one of your major strengths. If you're doing a job that involves little social interaction, such as research, Internet marketing, writing, or data analysis, you're going to be unhappy. You're like the fish trying to climb a tree.

On the other hand, if your job involves daily interaction with others, perhaps regularly presenting to an audience, or being in the front office, interacting daily with clients and customers, then you're going to enjoy your job because you're using your public speaking and communication talent frequently.

Peter Drucker, a famous author and management consultant said, *"Most Americans don't know what their strengths are. When you ask them, they look at you with a blank stare, or they respond in terms of subject knowledge, which is the wrong answer."*

I've tested this with my students and colleagues. Nine times out of ten when I ask someone what their strengths are, I'm faced with either a blank stare, or a response like "my strength is in (expertize, e.g. accounting)" and answers in terms of subject knowledge.

That said, let's look now at *how you can **use** your strengths* to your advantage. How can you get ahead in your career by using your strengths?

The Sage of Omaha, Warren Buffett, gives a great answer to this question. He recommends, *"Capitalize on your strengths and manage around your weaknesses."*

Notice what he doesn't say. Something we've been conditioned since school to do. He doesn't say, *"Focus and improve upon your weaknesses."* No, he says to *manage* them. When we focus only on our strengths, we're able to excel and become our best selves. If we focus on our weaknesses, then we only bring ourselves up to be average, like everybody else. Capitalize on your strengths, and then manage your weaknesses so they don't pull you back, and you'll start excelling in your career.

Let's look further at Warren Buffett for an example. If you read his famous Berkshire Hathaway letters, you'll see that he is a patient, long-term oriented, and practical man. These are his strengths. At a time when everyone was investing in Microsoft and every hot new technology company under the sun, instead of doubling down during this boom, Warren Buffet waited to see what was going to happen to this new thing called "the Internet." He was able to look ahead, noticed the market wasn't stable, decided to be patient, and refused to make an investment. As such, he didn't lose any money when the market for Internet stocks crashed in 2001. Trusting his strengths turned out to be a good bet.

How do you know if something is a strength of yours? Well here are three simple questions to ask:

1. Before doing the task, are you excited about it?
2. When doing the task, are you losing track of time. In other words, are you in flow?
3. When the task is complete, do you have more or less energy?

And, that's just one, quick and simple method. If you'd like another, more precise method to uncover and discover your strengths, visit this link: www.career10x.com/bonuses and get the free strength bonus gift I've created for you.

What Do You Have That No One Else Does?

The final element of your perfect job is to find your competitive advantage.

The bird can fly, the fish can swim, and the leopard can chase down its prey. These are the competitive advantages each animal has in the animal kingdom. It's the unique makeup of each animal that allows it to do what others can't.

Your career isn't as dramatic as the leopard's chase, but your competitive advantages are still important. They are a unique combination of your education, your experience, and your skills. If you combine these and use a little bit of creativity, you'll arrive at your competitive advantage. It's the edge that will allow you to get ahead of anyone else for a certain role or a certain position.

There is no unique place where you get these advantages. They can come from a variety of sources, from your schooling, mentors you've had, seminars you've attended, books you've read, previous jobs you've had, unique life experiences, accomplishments in your past, observations you've made, and so much more. It's essentially the sum total of your entire life and what makes you stand out. So it helps to really see the big picture. What has occurred in your life that could give you a competitive advantage?

When I was trying to take a leap from being a Brand Director to becoming a European Brand Director (a *huge* leap, because this was a game changing role), I took some time and looked through my past for any competitive advantages, the traits I had that made me better than anyone else for the position.

> **Education:** The first thing I looked at was my previous education. I was working in the business side of the life-sciences industry. This unique position had given me a variety in education and experience that was going to be helpful for the role. However, I wasn't the only one with this advantage. I had to look a bit deeper.

> **Experience:** This is what really made me stand out. Why? Because even though I was a Brand Director in a small market, it had been one of the first markets to launch this product worldwide. So I already had the necessary experience and insight into the market. I knew what worked and what didn't work. This was knowledge that

no one had at the European and Global headquarters. This would definitely give me an edge when applying for the job.

Skills: I already had marketing and leadership skills. I had proven myself in these areas to the organization, which someone from the outside would have had to do.

But it was really my previous experience of launching the same product in a smaller country that gave me the advantage I needed to land the role, which as you already now know, I did. Just think of this from the perspective of a hiring manager, you have a role to fill in for a product that needs to be successful in Europe, and right there you have a guy who intimately knows a product and has been successful with it in one of the countries. Perfect fit.

NARROW DOWN YOUR LIST OF PERFECT NEXT JOBS

We've already discussed the three critical elements of your perfect job. But that still isn't enough to actually find your perfect job.

Usually after my students have evaluated those three elements of their perfect job and have taken action they find:

- One to two areas in their organization that will give them high amounts of visibility. This is what I call "being in the right game."
- A list of their top five strengths.
- A list of experiences, education and skills that could give them a competitive advantage.

With this knowledge, it's time to generate a list of perfect job titles that fit the three criteria. It's almost like panning for gold.

When you pan for gold, you first find a good deposit location. These are usually streams located near mountains that have gold ore in them. Then you use your pan to scoop some gravel. Because gold is heavier than any other sediment, you look near the bottom of the pan for any gold. It's a three-stage process in which you continue narrowing it down until you've found the gold.

This is similar to determining your perfect job title. First we have to determine the elements that would make up your perfect job. Once we have that information, we can start looking for job titles and job descriptions that fit your criteria.

A great place to look for job titles would be your company's own Intranet. Look through the job descriptions and find the ones that fit your strengths, are in the right department, and in which you can get a competitive advantage.

Another great location to look for job titles is job search sites or on LinkedIn, mainly because the job descriptions are quite detailed on these sites, so there is a lot of information to help you determine if it will be a good fit for your criteria. Often all you need to do is to find several job titles that feel right (AFTER you've done all the previous steps I outlined) and read the first paragraph of the job description, which is usually a paragraph summarizing the purpose of the job.

The key here is that you're just searching for the job titles, not applying to them. These job adverts aren't for jobs you're going to apply to. This is just research to help you find the perfect job once you're ready for a promotion, which the other strategies in the book will get you ready for.

Validate Your Choice
And Choose A Winner

Remember the panning for gold analogy from above? Well, after you've scooped up the gravel, it's time to look for the gold. And that's what this section is about. Once you have a list of about five potential perfect jobs, it's time to get external validation to see if you have a winner.

Bob Pozen from Harvard University says, *"When you're on the job hunt, the best way to know if you want to work in a field is to simply talk to the people who do it."* So that's what you're going to do, too. It's very straightforward.

The key here is to find people who are in your perfect job, or have been in your perfect job, and find out from them what it's like.

The idea behind this is to make sure your vision of this perfect job matches the criteria you've found would be required for your perfect job. The last thing you want to do is to spend six months growing into your perfect job, only to find you hate it.

If you find some red flags or you don't have a good feel for the job description after talking to your colleague, then don't worry. You gained validation that the job title isn't for you. Cross it off your list and move on to the next one. Remember, you don't find gold on your first try; you have to keep trying. That's why you have a list of three to five potential perfect jobs.

To help you on this quest, I've put together some tips that will get you going in finding the right person to help validate your job position here: http://career10x.com/bonuses
If you do this, you'll be ahead of 95% of people in the workplace. The great majority of people never go to any effort to find out just what makes up the perfect job for them, nor do they ever

gain external validation. But if you do, then you've virtually guaranteed job satisfaction in your next job title. *Your perfect job title*. Doesn't that sound amazing?

CREATE A POWERFUL VISION AND FORCE IT TO WORK FOR YOU WHILE YOU SLEEP

By now you are actively working at securing your best chance at a fulfilling job and a successful career. But there is something else that can put the wind in your sails.

This part is all about putting the pieces together in your mind. It's about creating a **vision** that will serve as a magnet for your desires and your subconscious mind. It will pull you in the direction of your vision and will help you get all the actions, now or in the future, directed towards that one vision.

What do Gandhi, Martin Luther King Jr., and Nelson Mandela have in common? They all had a grand vision of what they wanted the world to be like. And they inspired others with this vision until it became a reality.

Having a vision, not just a goal, will make your mind work for you while you sleep. Your subconscious will process all the available information and plot out different scenarios while you're resting, so that day- after day, the action steps for you to get to your vision become more and more clear. We make better decisions after we've had a good night's sleep because of this. It's why we have the expression, "Let me sleep on it."

There are two elements to making this happen:

Visualize Like You're There

When Martin Luther King shared his "I have a dream" speech, he didn't talk in maybe's and what if's. He talked with certainty about his vision.

"I have a dream that one day this nation will rise up and live out the true meaning of its creed: 'We hold these truths to be self-evident, that all men are created equal.'"

Visualize the future of your perfect job, and make it feel real in your brain. Use present tense verbs when describing it to yourself. "I am a Sales Director" instead of "I want to be a Sales Director."

Every top athlete and business executive does this. They visualize the scenario they want until it's real. They will it into existence.

If you visualize your success to the point where your mind is convinced it's already won, you'll start making tiny, automatic decisions to bring about this victory. So take time to create the powerful vision that will turn into an invisible force pulling and directing you towards your perfect job.

Make It Visible Every Day

Apart from having this clear vision, you will need a visible reminder every day. Something you see daily that reminds you of your vision. It's all well and good making a clear and compelling vision that you want to step into, but if you forget about it, then you won't know where you're going.

Remember the saying, "out of sight, out of mind." It's the same for our visions of the future. So set up a daily reminder about your vision and never forget where you're heading.

You can find how I get my students to do this so that their minds can start working to get them to where they want - all on autopilot - here: http://career10x.com/bonuses

---

To Summarize:

- A perfect career consists of a series of perfect job titles.
- There are three elements to your next perfect job title: getting into the right game, knowing your strengths, and knowing your competitive advantages.
- Once you know this, use the Internet to find job descriptions that suit your criteria. Using this narrow down to five job titles that you'll like to pursue.
- Get external feedback to validate your choices. If a red flag comes up, move on to the next job title. When you find a job title that ticks all the boxes, congratulations, you've found your next perfect job title.
- Use visualization techniques to make your unconscious mind pull you forward to your destination.

Chapter 6

HOW TO FIND YOUR ONE BIG THING

Throughout this book I've hinted at the fact that you'll have to decide and work on your One Big Thing, but just what is it? What exactly do I mean when I refer to your One Big Thing?

I'll put it simply: Your One Big Thing is your flagship project. It is the initiative or project you choose to work on relentlessly over the next 6-12 months that will, in return, carry you over to your next job promotion. Why? Because if done correctly, your name will become synonymous with this exciting project. When people mention the One Big Thing, it'll always be in the same sentence as your name.

Let me illustrate this with a few examples.

Paris's One Big Thing

In the mid-19th century, Paris was facing a mini crisis; the city's citizens were slowly emigrating to live elsewhere in France and in Europe. Paris just didn't seem to have a focal point, something unique and exciting that lit up the imagination and drew in the crowds. London had Big Ben and Tower Bridge, Rome had the Colosseum, but Paris was not known for anything unique. It had a beautiful landscape and many famous landmarks, but nothing exciting and unique in the whole of Europe.

It was at this time that Gustave Eiffel, an architect who had already made a name for himself with his innovative bridge building techniques, came to the Champ de Mars, looked around at the vast empty expanse and thought, "*A huge tower would be great here. It'll be exciting, unique and will put Paris back on the map. It'll be a focal point for tourists and admirers.*" And the rest is history. The Eiffel Tower was unveiled to the world at the 1889 World's Fair, and ever since has become the iconic landmark representing Paris. It has drawn countless visitors from all over the world, reaping dividends for the city of Paris for over a hundred years.

Paris, of course, has a lot more to offer, but this one big landmark is what we all associate with the city, and it's the starting point for any Parisian tourist, and brings more attention to other city's sights.

The Eiffel Tower is not the only example of the One Big Thing. Think of famous art exhibitions in your city. What do you see advertised? The entire collection or one main piece? Of course, it's the latter. This one main piece creates interest and draws you in to then look at the rest of the exhibition. The Mona Lisa is a great example of this for The Louvre.

Before the advent of GPS, the first thing sailors looked for when approaching a port was the lighthouse, a tall tower built to draw sailors towards safe harbor away from the choppy sea.

Your One Big Thing will be your lighthouse, your Mona Lisa, your Eiffel Tower. It will be a project that will be the focal point of your work. When people ask how your work is going, they'll ask in detail about Your One Big Thing. When you're seeking advice from mentors, you'll talk about your One Big Thing. To put it simply, your One Big Thing will radically increase the value you bring to the workplace.

Remember…

Career Acceleration = Mindset x Value x Leverage.

Just as the Eiffel Tower increases the perceived value of Paris to the world, so will your One Big Thing increase your perceived value to your organization.

How To Make A Billion Dollars

But to show you the power of concentrating on your One Big Thing, I'll share a personal story.

When I became a European Brand Director in my organization, I'd chosen a product that needed turning around. If you remember from the previous chapter, this is one of two options I advise to choose when it comes to picking the right game, the other being an area of high growth.

The product had been projected to be our flagship product. It would bring in the majority of our revenue, and place us on the map in the market. When I say the majority, I mean $7 Billion in annual revenues.

It was going to be huge. Everyone in the company, from the CEO to the newly hired graduates, was excited for the product to be released.

And then the FDA didn't approve the product. This meant we couldn't sell it in the USA. We could still sell elsewhere in the world, but since the USA was our biggest market, it was a huge blow to the project.

Momentum fizzled out, and everyone lost their enthusiasm. No one believed in the product anymore. Everyone put their resources and energies elsewhere. This meant a product that was supposed to be our future rainmaker was instead generating a loss. It only made $40 Million in all of Europe.

That sounds like a lot of money, until you remember this product was supposed to bring in *billions of dollars*. We'd invested heavily because of this projection. The sales we were bringing in were a huge loss, less than 20% of our projections for the launch year.

A few months later, I became the European Brand Director of the product. I'd chosen it not only because of its potential, but because it really mattered to my boss. Also I had experience with this product. I had been in charge of launching this product in a smaller market, and it was a success. I knew this product could do really well if I could get everyone excited again.

However this was just the goal. I still didn't know *how* I was going to do this. This was when I decided to spend time to find my One Big Thing, the one project that I was going to work on to achieve my objective of turning around this product.

It took me three months to find my One Big Thing and this was okay. This is what I tell my students: some people will immediately know what their One Big Thing will be, and for others it will take some time to find it, maybe a week, or three months.

During those three months, I travelled across Europe and met with the other teams working on the product. I met with our customers and tried to get a picture of what was happening on the ground.

It was when I met with all the different teams in different parts of Europe that I realized we had a critical problem. We didn't have a clear strategy on how to market this product. Every team had their own ideas and their own method, but there was no clear, coherent approach. We didn't have a clear framework to guide everyone on how to market this product, instead everyone was just trying to see what works. This is a great way to work in a startup, but in an organization, it's the quickest way for a company-wide project to fail.

It was then when I realized what I should work on. I knew what my One Big Thing would be. I was going to create a unified marketing strategy for this product. It was going to be the "3 Golden Rules," an easy name to remember and a result of my deep dive into the market research done on the product. Based on the insights from my research, I was able to develop a detailed strategy on how to market the product, communicate it clearly to all the teams involved, and set the right key performance indicators.

I faced a lot of resistance at first, but I kept pitching the 3 Golden Rules. I made a logo and created a banner. I had it in the signature of all my emails. I talked about it to everyone who was related to the product. I asked for advice and feedback on it. In essence, I lived and breathed my One Big Thing. You couldn't think of Bozi without thinking of the 3 Golden Rules.

After a month I was able to convince one country to adopt the 3 Golden Rules. They immediately started to see success in their sales. And this was exactly what I needed. I knew if I could prove it worked once, others would adopt it. Now I had a case study, and I was ready to spread the 3 Golden Rules across the rest of Europe, and persuade senior executives to invest large amounts of money in my product. And they did.

Soon the product exploded and was flying off the shelves wherever I went.

In one and a half years, the product had gone from making $40 Million to $300 Million. Today the brand is worth $1.3 Billion in annual revenues. A brand that no one believed in is now a major money maker.

My One Big Thing hit the criteria that I'll share later on in this chapter. It solved one specific problem that our organization was facing. It was achievable within 12 months. The results were clearly measurable by the revenues of the brand. I lived and breathed the 3 Golden Rules, so it was inevitable that people attached my name to it. The problem really mattered to my boss and to the company.

And to think... if I hadn't made the 3 Golden Rules my priority, the one thing I worked on first thing in the morning for an hour, if I had said "Yes" to all the other projects people wanted me to join... then that product would still be making a loss and would be a disappointment to the company.

WHY YOU NEED A ONE BIG THING

Still not convinced that you need a One Big Thing? Well here's some news for you. This method is not only based on my experience and the experience of my students, but it's also grounded in psychology.

There's a small but important part of your brain called the reticular activation system, or RAS for short. This system is part of what governs your attention and focus. Harnessed properly, it can help you achieve your desires and dreams.

Your RAS is like an inner gatekeeper filtering all the information going in and out of your brain from all your senses. What makes it so special is that it subconsciously directs your attention to what it deems important. If you tell your brain to focus on triangles, all of a sudden you'll notice triangles everywhere.

This not only works with visual information, but with all sorts of information. Have you ever noticed that when you set yourself a goal, and you focus on that goal, you gradually start to notice things and make realizations that help you get closer to your goal? That's your RAS at work.

For example, have you ever been in a noisy environment like a busy airport terminal or a loud party, and then you hear your name, despite all the background noise? That's your RAS at work. Or when you dream about getting that new BMW 5 Series car, and you suddenly start to see it everywhere, in adverts, on the road...You notice people in your social circle who drive the car, and you wonder how you didn't notice before? That's your RAS.

This is why you need your One Big Thing. Once you focus on your One Big Thing, your RAS will switch on and start working for you. It'll notice resources and people who can help you with your One Big Thing. Also the RAS of other members in your organization will become tuned to you and your One Big Thing. They'll notice things in the world that are associated with your One Big Thing and its link to you. In both ways, it works to your advantage.

So how do you find time for your One Big Thing when you're already overwhelmed at work?

Well, first you need to learn to say "NO." Saying no is possibly one of the most important skills you can learn in your work and in life. Steve Jobs is a great example of this. He said, "My job is to say no to 19 out of 20 ideas so we can focus on what really matters." Today Apple is a multi-billion dollar company that makes money off what are essentially fewer than 10 products.

The opposite example of this is what our friend Ordinary Joe does. Joe says "YES" all the time at work. When his boss asks him to join another project, he says yes. When his colleagues ask him for time out of his day for advice or for a chat, he agrees. He accepts requests to meetings that contribute nothing towards his goals but take time and energy out of his day. Ordinary Joe spreads himself so thin that he ends up feeling overwhelmed and stressed out, without achieving anything tangible.

And at the end of the year when a new manager or worker enters the office, they'll ask, "Who's that person sitting at that desk?" pointing to Joe's desk. People will respond, "You mean Joe? Well he's the guy... Joe is Joe," maybe following up with his job title but that's where it'll end.

Joe becomes another anonymous cog in the organization, not known for anything special, anything that contributes to the success of the company or the success of his boss. He's a good guy (which is fine) and hardworking (which is commendable), but he's not known for a One Big Thing that matters, and that's why he will never stand out.

Why does Joe agree to everything? Joe wants to be successful, like the rest of us. He believes that the key to becoming successful is by not putting all of his eggs in one basket. He believes he'll increase his chances of succeeding if he works on any project that he has the opportunity to work on. It's almost like how buying more raffle tickets increases your odds of winning (but not by that much). He is led by the feeling of uncertainty and wants to somehow guarantee himself eventual triumph. However this is what psychologists call "scarcity-based thinking." Joe has been conditioned to believe that there are a limited amount of opportunities, and that he needs to do everything he can in order to ensure he'll succeed.

Extraordinary Jennifer, on the other hand, is a completely different animal. Jennifer understands the power of saying no in her career and says it 90% of the time. Of course she doesn't say an outright "No," which fosters hostility, she instead says it in a manner that encourages mutual respect. I'll give an example. Let's say your boss asks you to join one project after another. He just keeps burying you in more work and responsibilities. Saying no wouldn't be, "No can do, boss," instead it would be, "I have all these projects on my plate and I have a limited amount of hours during the day, so which ones should I focus on and prioritize?"

Extraordinary Jennifer also says no to her coworkers who are asking for advice, or for a quick chat over coffee. Jennifer wouldn't give them an outright rejection, but she would say, "Okay, sure, I'll love to help. However would Friday at 3pm work for you? And could you please send me a short note of what the issue is and what problems you're facing?" You see, Jennifer wants to help, but she offers to do it at the end of her work week. Why? Because Jennifer knows she can best help the organization by focusing on her priorities first, before helping someone else.

As a result, Jennifer is balanced. She isn't stressed or hurried. She isn't spread out. She's focused and happy at work. Furthermore Jennifer sets aside time each morning, one hour before email or anything else, where she works on her One Big Thing. At the end of the year, when a new person or manager walks into the office and asks, "Who is that person sitting at that desk?" while pointing at Jennifer, her colleagues usually respond, "Oh, you mean Jennifer? She's the person behind..." mentioning the project that is her One Big Thing. In other words, her name is attached to this successful, exciting and unique project that matters to the department and the company. She is a rock star and everyone knows it.

Think about everyday products you see everywhere and how they're attached to a name. For example, Volvo's One Big Thing is safety. When you think of Volvo, you think of safety, which is why it's extremely popular among families with children.

As I mentioned in my story, your One Big Thing might be immediately obvious to you, however it can also take a month or longer to identify it. And this is okay. Better to spend time identifying your One Big Thing that you'll work on for 6-12 months, than to waste all that time on a project that isn't inspiring or doesn't get you promoted.

Identifying your One Big Thing is a critical step in your Promotion. If done right, it can be the lead domino that starts getting you tangible results in your career. By tangible results I mean promotions. Lots of promotions. Salary raises? You bet.

If you'd like more help identifying your One Big Thing, visit this link to get a free worksheet and checklist I've created to help you: www.career10x.com/bonuses.

Name Your One Big Thing For Success

Do you know what Norma Jeane Mortenson, Lee Jun-fan and Stevland Hardaway Judkins have in common? Do you even recognize those names?

I bet you don't, but you sure would recognize their faces if I showed them to you. Why?

Because Norma Jeane Mortenson changed her name to Marilyn Monroe, Lee Jun-fan to Bruce Lee and Stevland Hardaway Judkins to Stevie Wonder.

Having the correct name for your brand is critically important, not just if you're a celebrity, but if you want your One Big Thing to be noticed and remembered by your colleagues and your organization.

The correct name can increase the value of your project so that it excites and energizes everyone who hears it, and position it to be extremely valuable to your company. Many people in the 90% crowd believe that "If I do a project really well, then it doesn't matter what it's called."

There can be nothing further from the truth.

In my industry and company, there are 20 people whose responsibilities lie with just naming products. This naming team consists of psychologists, lawyers, trademark people, and marketers... because large organizations understand how important the name of the product can be.

I'll give you a famous example about how changing the name and the cover of a book can make a huge impact. In 1982, an author named Nora Hayden published a book called *Astrological Love* with an uninspiring cover. The book content was great, but the title was awful, the cover cheesy, and it had a long and forgettable subtitle.

Sixteen years later, the same book, the *exact same book*, with none of the content changed, was republished after carrying out what is known in the marketing industry as "split testing." In 1998 the book was republished as *"How to Satisfy A Woman Every Time... and have her beg for more!"* and sold 2.5 Million copies.

That's how important a name can be.

For your One Big Thing, you have to create a name that is impossible to ignore or forget. I'll repeat that:

Create names that are impossible to ignore or forget.

There is so much more to be said on the topic of choosing the right name and branding it, but if you take one message from this part of the book, it is this - create names that are impossible to ignore or forget.

10 MINUTES A DAY TO MASTERY

Do you know the key part of any marketing or military strategy? It isn't how you're going to deceive the enemy, or how you're going to position yourself.

No, the most important part is where you're going to establish a beachhead.

For World War II it was on the beaches of Normandy that Eisenhower decided to concentrate the entire might of the allied forces. He knew that if they captured and established a base of operations on the beaches of Normandy, then they would be able to branch out and start the liberation of Europe.

For Apple, it was by focusing on creatives and the counterculture movement of the 1970s and 1980s that they were able to establish a raving fan base that would buy all their products, even if they were inferior to the competition.

But what does this have to do with your One Big Thing?

Well, it has to do with how you structure your day. When most people hear about a strategy to accelerate their career, they get excited and are motivated. They stop everything they're doing and focus on implementing the strategies over the next couple of days. However, this isn't sustainable. They get burned out, and they have to maintain balance with their responsibilities at work, as well as their social and home life.

It's the equivalent of wanting to chop down a tree, and grabbing the very first tool and trying to chop it down, whether that tool is a spade, a broom, or even a dull axe. You don't care because you're excited to chop down the tree. However, anyone watching would tell you that that's a stupid strategy. You're not likely to get the tree down that way anytime soon.

However consider what the smart lumberjack does.

> *"Give me six hours to chop down a tree and I will spend the first four sharpening the axe."*
>
> -Abraham Lincoln

The smart lumberjack front loads the work. They spend half or more of their time sharpening their axe. Why? Because they know that this is the more strategic option. This is the best use of their resources and will get them astonishing results.

So how can you apply this to your career acceleration?

It's simple. You spend 10 minutes of your day planning your career acceleration by focusing on your monthly and weekly goals and your career acceleration roadmap (you can develop the one on your own using the material from this book or use the one from my advanced course). You plan your day and how you're going to move forward on your One Big Thing.

It might not sound like a big deal, but believe me, this is the equivalent of sharpening your axe. This is the front loading that can reduce the amount of time you spend on work by 50% or more. If you don't spend 10 minutes in your workday focusing on your career acceleration, your momentum will stall, you'll feel overwhelmed, and you'll lose sight of the big picture. You'll lose motivation and soon be back at square one.

So why should you commit to the practice of starting your day with 10 minutes focused on your career acceleration?

Creates A Habit And Delivers Momentum

By assigning a few minutes at the beginning of your day towards your desired progress, you begin creating a habit and building momentum. Neuroscience and behavioral psychology tells us that it takes 20-30 days to create a habit. After 20 days you've built momentum, you've built a pathway in your brain that's easy to follow. Within two months you will feel like it's a part of who you are, and you won't understand how you used to start your day without focusing on the big picture.

Keeps Your Personal Career
Goals ABOVE Company Goals

This is critical. As I said in Chapter 1, no one in this world cares more about your career than you do. I'll repeat that because it's important: *No one cares about your career more than you do.* Many smart people, smart but still in the 90% crowd, expect everyone else in the company to pay more attention to their career: HR, their Manager, and the CEO. That's impossible. Just think about the number of people HR oversees. How many people is your manager responsible for, Including himself and the CEO? Like I said, impossible. Don't make the same mistake.

By starting the day focusing on the big picture of YOUR career acceleration, you're keeping your personal goals above the company's goals, which is a win-win for everyone. It's by advancing in your career, by focusing on your One Big Thing, that you can bring the most value to your company, which aligns with their goals.

It's not selfish. Your company can only get the best out of you once you start focusing on your personal goals.

It Puts Your Career Direction In Your Hands

By starting your day with your big picture plan, you are taking control of your career's direction. Think about the first thing a ship captain does when he enters the bridge. The first question out of his mouth is, "What is our heading?" That's it. Why? Because the ship's direction is the most important thing to the captain. If he doesn't pay attention to this, then the currents can carry the ship in the wrong direction.

When you focus on your career acceleration every day, you'll be able to direct the ship that is your career in the direction you want. You'll gain a sense of control over your destiny. And you'll be more motivated to give your all during the workday.

Feel Accomplished Before You Even Start Your Day

Have you ever had those days where, after eight hours at work it's time for you to go home, and then you sit and wonder, "Wait... what did I accomplish today?" And then you realize you've actually not been able to get anything done, except maybe clear your Inbox?

Well, with this habit, you'll never feel like that again. Instead, you'll feel a sense of accomplishment before your day has even started. You'll know that step-by-step, day-by-day, you're taking your career under your control. You'll know that you're slowly entering the 10% club, and that you're making real, tangible progress in your career.

Ninety percent of people don't start their day like this. Ordinary Joe's day goes like this: He starts his day by making a cup of coffee (nothing wrong with that). He then turns on his computer, which is his first mistake. Once his computer is up and running, he logs on and starts going through his emails for the next 90 minutes, responding and reading emails. His usual response is something along the lines of, "I'll get on that, but I have 350 emails in my Inbox, and I'm really busy," which is another way of trying to communicate, "I'm so important."

After these 90 minutes, Ordinary Joe feels accomplished. But what did he really do? He just responded to 300 emails, and what did that accomplish? Did it move a critical project forward? Did it set off a chain of events that will deliver millions of dollars of revenue down the line? Or did he just respond with one sentence answers that didn't really accomplish anything but let everyone know, "Hey there, I'm alive, and I'm working in the office today!"

Ordinary Joe has confused activity with accomplishment. Checking his email is an activity, not an accomplishment. He hasn't done anything related to his One Big Thing, or related to his career acceleration. Instead his career is stagnating, he's still in the same square that he started in, and he has no control over where he's heading.

However... if you do your research and see what successful people do at the start of their days, whether in the corporate world, entrepreneurs, personal development consultants, heads of famous charities, political figures, anyone who has reached a certain level of success, you'll see that all of them have powerful daily habits which they refer to as their "rituals."

Extraordinary Jennifer has a powerful ritual at the start of her day. First she buys or makes her coffee (often people like Jennifer buy a premium coffee, starting their day off on a high note). Then Jennifer reviews her roadmap and her weekly goals WITHOUT looking at her computer. Why? Because she knows that the moment she turns on her computer she'll become distracted, especially if she doesn't have a goal to start with. Remember your Reticular Activation System, you want to direct your attention and focus towards your career road map and to your weekly goals.

Next, Jennifer spends the next single hour focusing on her One Big Thing. Why? Because this is the project she's chosen to relentlessly focus on for the next 12 months. She knows if she creates a tangible result with this project, she'll rapidly accelerate her career and increase her reputation. She creates a daily habit, a ritual of working on her One Big Thing. It matters to her company, to her boss, her team, and to her. So she focuses on it.

Then afterwards, as a result of this, she has a sense of accomplishment. A real accomplishment, not just empty activity. She has accomplished something and it wasn't by reacting to someone else's emails, but by her being proactive. She has put a tiny dent in the universe. She's progressing her career one step at a time, and she's in control. She's not letting anyone else stand in the way of her goals.

So how do you do that? How do you start your day by being proactive and by making a tangible step forward in your career? Well, you've already blocked out the first 10 minutes of your day on your calendar for your career acceleration (so you create a habit of putting your career first). Next, spend these 10 minutes working on your One Big Thing.

> **To Summarize:**
>
> - Your One Big Thing is the flagship project you'll work on for the next 6-12 months that will radically raise your profile in your organization and deliver tangible value.
> - After identifying your One Big Thing, which can take up to three months, you need to name and brand it so that it attracts attention.
> - Spend 10 minutes of your day on career acceleration and working on your One Big Thing BEFORE anything else. Extend this to one hour when you've started to build momentum. This will ensure you place your career goals above your company's goals, and you'll feel in control of your career.

Now that you've started to identify your One Big Thing, it's time to start growing your influence. It's time to learn how to make your boss work for you.

Chapter 7

MAKE YOUR BOSS WORK FOR YOU

Remember that there are three elements in your overall Career Acceleration,

Career Acceleration = Mindset x Value x Leverage.

Now that you know the mindset required to enter the 10% club and how to increase your value, it's time to learn how to gain leverage. You're going to do that by growing your influence.

What do I mean by influence? Influence can mean many things to different people. However, when it comes to your Career Acceleration, I want you to think of influence as the following:

> *"Influence is the ability to get people to do what you want them to do, but for the reasons they come up with themselves or for the reasons they already have."*
> - Tony Robbins

From here on in, you're going to learn how to get people to accelerate your career, but for *their* own reasons. You'll be tapping into the underlying psychological factors that all people of influence know on a near subconscious level.

And the first person you'll need to learn how to influence will be your boss.

The Goal Is Not To Get Along With Your Boss, The Goal Is To Get Your Boss To Work For You

Notice this chapter bears the title, *Make Your Boss Work For You*, not, *Make An Ally With Your Boss* or a clickbait blog headline like, *How to Get Along With Your Boss.* Why? Because these are surface solutions to a deep problem. Getting along with your boss isn't going to secure your promotion, nor is making an ally out of your boss.

No, in order to enter the 10%, you need to get your boss to work for you. The real success comes when someone who is powerful and influential is working for you and your next job promotion.

I'll warn you, from my experience and the experience of some of my students, some of the principles in this chapter may turn your world upside down. Some of the things may be really counter-intuitive, make you feel uncomfortable, and may take you out of your comfort zone.

But as we've talked about it before, growth happens outside your comfort zone.

And you might become addicted to this growth like my student Monika...

HOW MONIKA CHANGED THE GAME WITH HER BOSS

For most people, three months is just a change of season in their climate, but not for Monika. For Monika, that is how long it took her to go from a struggling HR manager to being a highly prominent HR Director for Central Eastern Europe, on the radar of key influential people in her organization.

Talk about a change of season.

But first, a bit more about her background. Monika had been an HR Professional for 18 years, and was working for a very large Fortune 500 company. She also has an ambitious and competitive character, like most people who enroll in my course. Yet, where she truly stands out compared to my other students is her incredible ability to instantly take action after learning something new. She is living proof that action is where the magic happens. When I asked how she did at school, Monika confessed to being a very competitive person. She was always first or second at school, and was unhappy when she was second.

So you can imagine how she felt when she was passed over for promotion.

Passed Over For Promotion

Monika had been eyeing a very specific job promotion for some time when suddenly, that very position was open and needed to be filled. To her colleagues and anyone in the know, it was obvious that Monika was the right choice; she had the experience, had been in the organization for a long time, and was more than smart enough for the role. However, the position went to a recently hired colleague instead.

Monika was deeply disappointed for a little while. Her colleagues tried to comfort her, but the choice affected Monika on a deeper level. This was where her competitive spirit worked against her. She experienced a drop in her self-esteem, and she started asking herself questions like, "Am I really progressing my career? Am I as good as I think I am?", Monika wasn't down for long. She bounced back emotionally after a few days and started taking productive steps to solve her problem. She credits this quick change in spirits to her extensive life experience.

Monika started asking herself the same questions as before, but not as a way to bring herself down, but to objectively analyze what she was doing wrong. She started wondering if there was something she wasn't doing well enough to get promoted, or if there was something she didn't understand. Perhaps she was coming across to senior leaders in her organization as someone who was unpromotable. Yet Monika's problem was simple. She didn't have the right relationships with her boss or her mentors.

Monika was facing another typical challenge, her boss was located far away from her office. I'm not talking about someone 10 miles away, but someone who worked in a different country. She couldn't just casually bump into them in the cafeteria. As I've said before, in your career, if you're out of sight, you're out of mind.

Eye Opener

Two months later, Monika came across my free online training. Intrigued, she decided to attend.

In my training, I offer a simple solution on how to get promoted rapidly in your career, similar to the one in this book. Monika was curious, not only for her own career advancement, but for the responsibilities involved in her profession. Working in HR, some of her duties involved advising her colleagues in their careers, so she decide to invest in her knowledge by attending my webinar. Even though it was held at 1:30 am in her time zone, she woke up in the middle of the night just to attend. Talk about ambition!

Convinced by what she learned during the webinar, she decided to enroll in my Career Acceleration Formula course, and her mind was blown.

"The course really opened my eyes. In the first couple of hours I realized that I wasn't exposed to the right people in the organization."

Monika sent me an email and asked if I could coach her. I don't offer 1:1 coaching, but there was something about her determination that made me jump on a call with her the next day. During our call I asked her a simple question, "What's your relationship with your manager?" Monika explained how it was almost non-existent. She also mentioned that her manager just started at a new role and was facing multiple challenges, one of which was that her whole team is remote. Monika also felt she didn't have any particular reason to reach out to her.

I knew from my experience the answer that Monika needed.

"Monika, wake up. It's your job to make your boss's life easier! Now tell me, what can you specifically do to help her?"

Monika said this triggered an important insight in her, like someone turning a light switch on. She realized that if she didn't make an effort to reach out, to inform her boss what she was up to and to understand how she could help her boss, she wouldn't be able to even begin to think about advancing her career. Monika would become another anonymous cog in the organization.

Monika came to understand that she had to start connecting with her managers and senior leaders, or she wouldn't get her perfect job. She realized her role wasn't to sit and wait for a miracle to happen, but to be active and responsible for her situation. She later went on would say, *"it clicked in my mind that I shouldn't feel like a victim, but that I should sit behind the wheel of my career and to drive it to where I wanted."*

She reached out to her new manager and arranged for a few face-to-face meetings. There was an instant connection. It was no longer just a professional relationship, but one of close friendship and mutual support. Monika empathized with the dual-role of her boss's new position. After just a few hours with her boss, Monika found specific ways to help. First, she offered her manager help in learning about the company's culture. Second, she offered to help manage several members of the team who were local for her (but were remote for her boss). In other words, Monika went from a highly passive, low visible role, to taking charge.

Monika's mindset wasn't, *"How can I meet and talk to my manager for my benefit?"* Instead it was, *"How can I help her do her job? What can I offer that would solve her challenges?"* She focused on her manager instead of herself, a key mindset I shared in Chapter 4.

Monika was amazed; she didn't realize that she could have a relationship of mutual trust and support with her manager. She also didn't realize the opportunities it would later open her up to. To start with, her manager offered her the chance to meet senior leaders in the organization and to see what else the organization was working on. Monika began networking with these senior leaders and others who had her job role in different departments of the organization. She used every opportunity she could to connect with people. She made herself available for meetings whenever she could, and made sure to have lunch or coffee with leaders in different departments.

Monika started to visibly expose herself to her organization, building up influence to leverage her brand, her brand being herself.

One day, Monika travelled for personal reasons and was, coincidentally, closer to the organization's headquarters. By close I mean 60 miles away. She used the opportunity to connect with her boss's boss, who had offered to go to lunch if she was ever nearby.

During this meeting, Monika was asked what her aspirations were for the next quarter. Because of my course, she was already well prepared and had an answer ready. They had a great engaging conversation discussing Monika's goals and her strengths.

Two days later, *only two days later*, Monika was offered a chance to work on a project that aligned with her goals. This was the first signal that she was being prepared for the position she ultimately wanted.

A few weeks later, Monika was offered her new role, cross-division HR Head for Central Eastern Europe, a major leap in her career.

It's All About Connections

When I asked Monika what she'd learned from the experience, she heavily emphasized the power of connecting with others and its impact on one's career. *"Look for ways to add value to your boss and to other important stakeholders."* By paying it forward, you ensure that people will reciprocate in helping with your career. Also, by always looking for opportunities to connect with others, you make yourself visible and expose yourself to the organization. Who is more likely to get promoted, the person who is visible and takes as many chances as they can get to connect with the relevant people in the organization, or the person who is stuck in their department and never leaves to meet anyone, apart from their immediate colleagues?

It's a simple choice. So make sure you're in the former category.

I could tell that Monika was smart and ambitious, but what I didn't know was how she was already looking forward to more responsibilities that she could take on.

When I asked Monika how the Career Acceleration Formula course helped with her career, this is exactly what she said, with a smile (I was a bit shocked, to tell you the truth):

"Career Acceleration Formula is the first step-by-step prescription for career success. It is something you can get addicted to at some point. It's something that works, so why not try it?"

WHY YOU NEED YOUR BOSS (HINT: IT'S NOT WHAT YOU THINK)

For a moment I want you to picture something. Something that might seem impossible now, but bear with me. Suspend your disbelief for a moment and picture this:

Imagine your boss working for you. Imagine your boss going to other hiring managers in your organization during the day and telling them how great you are, how amazingly successful your projects are, how sharp you are, how great of a team player you are. Imagine your boss doing that over the course of one day. Now imagine him doing that every single day. How amazing would that be?

Wouldn't it be almost like your boss was working for you? Wouldn't that influence your career and catapult it into the stratosphere?

I'm here to tell you that the fantasy can be real. It isn't too far from what people with extraordinary careers experience. In 2005 two researchers, James Citrin and Richard Smith, interviewed over 16,000 people with extraordinary careers and here is what they found out:

"Extraordinary people don't climb to the top; they are carried there by the people who work for them."

Did you catch that? People in the 10% club don't grapple and climb over their peers to get to the top. It isn't a race or a competition to determine the survival of the fittest. No, people in the top 10% are **carried** by the people who work for them. Not just your team members, but anyone who is **working for** your job promotion.

Remember earlier on when I shared my story? I can tell you one of the most critical elements that determined the success of my early career was precisely my relationship with my boss.

In my first job as an entry-level sales representative, I was purely focused on results, and didn't have any kind of relationship with my boss. That resulted in me being fired after only a simple mistake on my part.

In my second job, I focused purely on relationships, but not in an effective manner. I did everything you're not supposed to do if you want to experience career acceleration. I tried to please everyone, I said yes to all the projects, but my relationship with my boss was neutral. It wasn't negative, but it wasn't positive. After a year, I left because I knew I wasn't going anywhere, and it wasn't the right environment.

But in my third job (and in every job after that), I focused from day one on *managing my boss*. It was my bosses who actively helped me go from being a Junior Brand Manager to being a Senior Global Product Director in a few years. I was promoted six times in six years with a 15x increase in salary. All thanks to my bosses. Why? Because I learned how to understand them better and build relationships from the beginning. In fact, some of them are still good friends of mine. They've written public and private letters of recommendation for me, and whenever I'm up for a promotion, all of my previous bosses *go out of their way* to talk me up to hiring managers.

Still not convinced?

Well, just imagine the opposite. Imagine that you didn't have your boss working for you. What are the alternatives? Two come to mind.

First, your boss could be indifferent about you. She could just see you as another anonymous team member at an indistinct desk. When it comes time for you to get promoted, what will she tell the hiring managers?

"..."

Nothing. She'll tell them absolutely nothing. Or she might say some empty corporate speak when specifically asked what she thinks of you, but it'll be essentially nothing. You might as well play the sound of crickets chirping to the hiring manager, that'll be just as effective as what your boss will say.

The second alternative is worse; this is where your boss dislikes you. He dislikes your attitude at work and thinks you're a waste of company resources. What will he say when asked by a hiring manager about his opinion of you when you're up for promotion?

Actually he won't need to be asked because he'll start actively blocking your upward moves. "Oh Joe? He is not ready, there is a LOOONG way forward for him and I think you need someone who can jump on board fast."

Clearly, these are two scenarios you don't want.

The real power in your career acceleration comes from others endorsing you. This is a form of social proof, and is one of the most powerful tools out there that will persuade someone to take action.

What is social proof? Imagine you've just driven to a new town at night. Your phone is out of battery and you're hungry. As you're driving through town, you come across two local restaurants on opposite sides of the street. One of the restaurant's parking lots is empty even though the restaurant is open. The other restaurant has a few cars in its parking lot; you can see clearly through the windows that quite a few people are eating there.

Now which restaurant will you choose?

If you're like most people in the world, you'll opt for the latter. That's social proof in action. You'll choose the restaurant that has more people in it, as they must know something you don't. (In fact, even if your phone was charged, you'll probably have checked for online recommendations, which are another form of social proof.)

That's the power of having your boss endorse you. Hiring managers, when looking for someone to fill a role, will look at candidates who have endorsements, who have a form of social proof.

There's something I call the Influence Ladder. I call it a ladder because there are four levels and in order to get to the top rung of the ladder. you have to get past the lower ones.

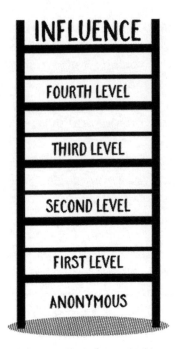

Figure 12: The Influence Ladder

First Level: <u>You're</u> talking about your One Big Thing, and through the power of association and the halo effect, if your project is great, your boss and everyone around you thinks of you as great. An example for this is when you go to the head of sales and ask for advice on how to position your One Big Thing. He'll give you some tips, and as you leave he'll think "Hmmm, that project looks exciting. That guy is really going places."

As great as this level is, it's not enough to get you in the 10% club. You have to keep climbing the ladder.

Second Level: This is where <u>your boss is verbally</u> supporting you. When asked by his colleagues and hiring managers, he has nothing but positive things to say about you. He may also actively go out of his way to recommend and endorse you. This is a great place to be, but you can go even further.

Third Level: This level, which is more fun and more impactful to your career, is where <u>your boss</u> puts down the fact that you're awesome <u>in written form</u>. There's something magical about having a statement written down. It formalizes it, and makes it tangible. It's why the very basis of contract law for millennia is that there must be a written contract formalizing the agreement (or a third party to serve as witness).

At this level, your boss has written in your career development plan (often an official HR kind of document) that you're ready for the next job role. She recommends a specific job role and lists the reasons you're ready. This is a powerful document, because if she writes it, then she really means it. Publicly.

Fourth Level: This is the ultimate level, and the level I want you to reach. This is when others are talking about how great you are. You're constantly being evangelized by your colleagues and your bosses to anyone who'll listen. They're not talking about how great your project is; <u>they're talking about how great *you* are</u>. This creates momentum in your reputation, and will make you an incredibly influential person in the organization. This is the level where others start competing against each other to recruit you, throwing salary increases at you, bonuses, perks, and stock options.

But how do you get your boss to give you this level of endorsement? How can you get this level of influence?

In movies, a character only gets this amount of influence by holding some kind of leverage over their boss, something they can blackmail them with. But in real life, you can get this kind of influence through far more ethical means.

The kind of means you'll learn about in this chapter.

THE FOUR PRINCIPLES

There are four very important principles you need to know and understand in order to gain influence in your career. These principles don't change. They are like the four seasons, fixed and out of your control. You can't change them, but if you work with them you'll gain rapid success:

1. You Can't Progress In Your Career Without Your Boss

This is so important, I'll repeat it: You can't progress in your career without your boss. Remember the quote earlier on, people who get to the top don't climb their way there, but are carried by those working for them? Well, whether you want to advance in your company or another company, you can't do it without being "carried" by your boss.

Decades ago, you could travel to a new country and get a second chance at rebuilding your reputation, but not today. The world is more transparent. People can check your LinkedIn profile, they can find your online gaming profile (linked to your Facebook) and see what your preferences are. People can see the blogs you comment on. Your preferences and behavior can be inferred by anyone willing to do a tiny amount of homework.

So don't try to game the system. Don't lie about your previous work experience, or about your boss's character. I personally know people who tried to do it and they had some mild success for two or three years, but then they ended up miserable. They never built anything tangible in their career, or moved around much. Think long term: You need your boss. If you can't live with this fact, then just start your own business.

2. No Matter How Bad It Looks, Every Boss Has Positive Intentions

Now the good news. Guess what? Your boss, who seems impersonal and maybe a bit aloof? He's actually a good guy inside.

I can already hear the cry, *"Bozi you don't know what you're talking about! People work out of self-interest. All hail Charles Darwin!"*

You know, I get it. This took me years to understand and to embrace. I learned this when I undertook Neuro-Linguistic-Programming (NLP) training some years ago, and I didn't believe it. I knew so many instances where people used tricks and were acting purely out of self-interest. Instances where people were mean, petty, and jealous. How on earth could they have had a positive intent?

Here is the truth, everyone is doing the best they can with the resources they've got. Read that again. When I say resources, I mean things like knowledge, emotional intelligence, and self-awareness. People's behavior often manifests itself as negative, but the underlying motivation (if you dig deeper) is usually a positive one (remember, they are doing the best they can). For example, let's say someone is mean to you because they fear you and want to protect their position. Ask yourself, "Why do they want to protect their position?" Maybe because their position provides them with status and money. But why do they want that? Well, maybe it's to impress that woman they've always had their eye on, or maybe because they need their job to pay their kids' tuition fees. Whatever it is, people are doing the best they can and the underlying motivation is a positive one.

Once you understand and realize this, you'll see that there is always something positive that you can relate to. Something that you can use to build a relationship. A relationship that will change your career.

3. Becoming A Master Of Psychology Will Take You Far

This point is crucial and related to the previous one. You need to become a master of psychology. Just as a software developer needs to understand and master a programming language to build software, you as a human being need to understand the software that all humans run on. It'll take you far in your career, as everything you could possibly want is in the hands of someone else. If you understand psychology, you'll understand how to persuade them to provide you with what you want (hint, you usually have to provide what they want, in exchange).

Spend time understanding what words mean, understanding your language, improving your language. Learn to make more impact with your words. Talk in benefits and not features. Learn how to read between the lines. Learn what makes people tick, how to quickly make friends, or to quickly build trust. If you do this, you'll go really far not only in your career, but in life.

4. Being A Yes Person Doesn't Work Because You'll Lose Respect

If you are constantly being a "yes person" to your boss, in front of your colleagues, if you are constantly jostling to sit next to your boss in meetings, and to be the main topic of conversation, if you are constantly doing all these things the 90% crowd believe is the key to success... then you'll lose respect. It's that simple.

The key here is to provide a "pattern interrupt." This is something I also learned from NLP (and later in other areas of psychology, just under a different name) and it's effective.

What this means is when it comes to your boss, don't just say yes. Don't always agree with everything she says. Now I'm not saying disagree with everything, for example if she comes to you and asks for your help on a big project, and it helps her achieve her goals, it is important and urgent, fits your job description and your One Big Thing, then do it. But dare to challenge your boss, and challenge others when you don't agree. Speak up. It's quite natural to challenge opinions.

I want to make this clear; you're not doing this to engineer a reaction. You're doing this to authentically interrupt the pattern. And what's the pattern you're interrupting? Just think for a second. What is an influential boss used to? She is used to "yes men." That's the pattern. Become a "yes man" and you will become invisible. Authentically stand behind your opinions, and you will instantly attract attention in a positive way, even if people disagree with you.

Say yes when you mean yes; say no when you mean no. If you do this, people will never know what you're going to say next. You'll be interrupting the pattern, and you'll also get to state your opinions. This is important, because not only will it win you respect, you'll be known as someone who has an opinion, as opposed to a "yes man." Guess who management will turn to when they want ideas? They go to the person who has opinions.

Being sleazy and a "yes man" doesn't work; you'll lose respect. Be authentic, and be someone who interrupts patterns and stands out. It'll bring you results.

SEEING THE WORLD THROUGH YOUR BOSS'S EYES

Perspective is everything.

Your perspective determines your perspective, how you see the world, how you construct a map of the world around you. Therapists like to talk about our perspective as a pair of colored glasses. If we change our glasses, we can see the world in a different light.

If you change your perspective to see the world through your boss's eyes, you will see a radical shift in your career. It can put you on such a fast track, you'll be blown away! It's a long-term skill, but something that can be learned right away.

Figure 13: The Young Old Woman - W. E. Hill - British Cartoonist first published in 1915 in Punch Magazine

Here is a famous drawing we can use to illustrate the power of perspective. Tell me, when you see that drawing, what do you initially see? Write it down on a piece of paper.
What is the answer?

What would you say if I told you that 50% of respondents tell a different answer from the other 50%?

Half the people who see this picture say they see a young woman looking over her shoulder, away from the viewer.

The other half see an old woman looking down.

Look back at the drawing again and see if you can spot the other image in the picture.

Perspective matters. A subtle shift in perspective can completely change how you see the world. And guess how we process information? Through our perspectives. And it's this information that we act on.

If you can take a small amount of time and make the effort required to understand another person's perspective, your career will rapidly shift. It's not just a skill that will take you far in your career, but in your life.

In Dale Carnegie's timeless classic, *How To Win Friends and Influence People,* you find this piece of wisdom:

> *"The man who can put himself in the place of other men, who can understand the workings of their minds, need never worry about what the future has in store for him."*
> - Owen D. Young.

Just to put that in context, Owen D. Young's resume reads like a man born with the stars aligned in his favor. He was born on a small farm and rose to become a superstar lawyer, and then the President of General Electric. He also created the Radio

Corporation of America (RCA) and was a diplomat who served in the Second Reparations Committee after World War I.

But Owen D. Young credits his success to that simple shift in perspective. He was able to put himself in the place of other men, to understand their standpoint, the workings of their minds, and use that to his advantage.

So let's see how Ordinary Joe goes about treating his boss, i.e. how the 90% fail to change their perspective to see the world through their boss's eyes.

First, Joe does something that is career suicide; he trashes his boss behind his back. This is something many people do. They believe that it's okay to gossip, and it'll go unnoticed. But this couldn't be farther from the truth. Rumors and gossip spread faster than the flu, especially with today's instant communication technologies. All it takes is for the boss to be accidentally sent a message not intended for him, or for him to accidentally walk in on a water cooler conversation where he was the topic of conversation, for him to hear this piece of gossip. And you can be assured, he'll know who it was from.

And I'm not just talking about at work, but also over social media. It's the easiest thing for your boss to run a Google search for your name and to see what you Tweet. Don't be that guy.

Another thing Joe fails to do is to see his boss as a real human being. He only sees the job title, and the intimidating powers of it. He fails to see that his boss is a genuine human being with genuine human feelings who usually acts out for good reasons. When he is cracking the whip, it's not because he hates Joe, it's because he is worried about the project.

The third thing Joe does is blame his boss as the source of all his problems. According to Joe's perspective, everything wrong at work stems from his boss. This is something I've seen in the work environment all the time. People love to enter into "victim mode" and talk about what their boss did to them and how they are the target of injustice.

But the problem is, just by using this language, by mentally positioning themselves as inferior and helpless, they are creating a self-fulfilling prophecy. This mindset colors their actions, so that they *become* inferior and helpless. It's a cycle of decline and can create a state of learned helplessness.

How do you stop it? Don't blame your boss or anyone in your life as the source of your problems. It's your life. You have free will. You get to make your own choices every single moment of every single day. If you adopt this mindset, it'll give you such a sense of control that you can't help but seize the reins of your destiny.

The final thing Joe fails to do is that he doesn't even bother to try and understand the perspective of his boss. He doesn't bother taking 60 seconds to try and put himself in his shoes and ask, "why is he doing that?"

After all of this, Joe still expects to be promoted. He'll tell his colleagues and his manager, "I've been in this role for four years. I should get promoted because it's what I deserve..."

Seriously? He expects to get promoted with that attitude? If this sounds like what you've been doing, then stop. Trust me. You won't go far in your career if you adopt an attitude of being entitled to a promotion.

Now what does Extraordinary Jennifer do? What do the 10% do?

First of all, Jennifer understands that all people are people. That outside of work her manager has hobbies, interests, and the normal everyday worries, hopes, fears, and dreams that all people have. She understands that when her boss is angry, it's because they feel a lack of control, and are trying to exert some influence in this chaotic world. She empathizes with everyone.

Second, Jennifer constantly puts herself in other people's shoes. Whenever she is about to make a request, she spends a few minutes thinking about the other person, about their wants, needs, goals, and fears. This simple exercise means she gets what she wants most of the time. Why? Because she structures her request so that it's of benefit to them.

I'll give you an example. In 2001, when Arnold Schwarzenegger was starting his political career, he wanted to implement Proposition 29 in California. It was a simple proposal, to provide after school programs for teenagers. Studies had found that the hours just after school and before parents arrived home from work were the most dangerous moments in a teenager's life, they were unsupervised, and in areas of high crime this could lead to joining gangs, getting into drugs, and committing crime. By providing after school programs, teenagers get off the streets and take up more rewarding extracurricular activities.

The only problem? This bill needed government funding to work. Adding government programs is something that is against the core of Republican beliefs, and Arnold Schwarzenegger needed the support of the Republicans to ensure the bill passed.

So he took some time and thought about the issue. What was the number one concern of Republican lawmakers? Then it struck him. Republicans care about fiscal responsibility; about ensuring that government spending doesn't become irresponsible.

Using this knowledge, Arnold Schwarzenegger reframed the issue as a fiscal one. His pitch was as follows, you may think I'm asking you to spend an extra $420 Million, but in fact I'm asking you to save $1.3 Billion. By implementing this program, we'll actually be saving money later because of fewer arrests, fewer teenage pregnancies, and less neighborhood trouble. Studies show that for every dollar we spend on after school programs, we save three dollars down the line.

The result? The Republicans in California did something that many thought was impossible; they unanimously voted to implement and fund a new government program.

This is the power of putting yourself in someone else's shoes. By just taking one or two minutes to think about the other person and what they want and fear, you'll be able to frame your request in a manner that benefits them, and will increase the chances of their agreement.

Adjusting Your Style

In order to master career acceleration you have to go even deeper. You have to not only understand the other person's point of view, but you have to adjust your style. Understand, you adjust your style, not manipulate and engineer a response from your boss. When you adjust your style, your communication becomes more effective, and your actions speak louder than before.

But how do you do this?

This is one topic where there is a lot of misinformation out there on the Internet. Let me show you an extract from an actual article that is on the front page of Google for, "How to adapt to a new boss:"

"Make a good first impression. First perceptions are always important..."
(No shit. Make a good first impression. Of course I'd make a good first impression, I'm not an idiot.)

165

"Accept and adapt. Perhaps the surest way to make a good start with a new supervisor is to simply accept him or her in the role and be willing to adjust your work style as needed to ensure a productive relationship."
(Wait, what does that even mean?! Of course I should adapt, that's obvious, but how do I do it? How do I go about doing it?)

This is why going to the Internet for career advice isn't wise. In fact, it's quite simple to adapt and change your style to suit your boss. You don't have to be gimmicky or manipulative. You just need to understand basic psychology. I'll illustrate this with a personal story.

In one of my previous roles, one thing that was a source of growing dissatisfaction between my boss and I was how I would ask him questions and to make decisions. I would often ask him questions "on the fly," just as they popped into my head. I would come to a meeting and ask him for a big decision without sharing any information with him up front. This had been okay in my job title beforehand, but I could tell that my current manager was becoming frustrated with this behavior. He didn't explicitly say anything, but I could tell by his body language that it was a source of contention.

Knowing that this would hinder my progress at work, I took some time out and read a book called *Please Understand Me* (great title by the way), and I was exposed to different personality types. I took two simple tests, one for me and one for my boss, and found out that I was an extrovert and my boss was an introvert. It's a common misconception that extroverts are social and introverts are shy. It simply means that introverts get more energy from solitude, and extroverts from human interaction.

Now a fundamental difference between these two personality types is that extroverts are often talking while they're thinking, they are happy to improvise and give you an answer in one moment, and give you another down the line. However, introverts are different. When they say something, it means that they have given it some serious thought. They've spent the time to research and formulate a response, and once they say it, they won't change their response.

Of course my boss was frustrated! I was asking him for questions and to make decisions without giving him the time to think about it. This is something I'd been happy to do if I was in his place, but not him. And that's okay. So I decided to make one simple change. Just one, and it was very effective.

I decided to give him information before I asked for any decision, small or big. I would send him some information to digest and give him time to answer before I made a request. The result was that I started getting better answers, and no frustration on his end. After some time, he came and let me know that he really appreciated the adjustments I'd made in my communication style. This was amazing, because it was a simple change. Just one change. No manipulative techniques, no framing gimmicks. Just taking full charge for the outcome of my communication instead of making myself a victim.

MAKE YOUR BOSS PLAN IT ALL OUT FOR YOU

This is a powerful strategy. Here you'll learn how to use the influence principle known as "Consistency/Commitment." You'll use this principle to get your boss to plan your next stop, your next job title, and get it in written form.

I first learned about the Consistency/Commitment Principle, (which we'll call the C/C Principle from now on) from Dr. Robert B. Cialdini's bestselling book, *Influence: The Psychology of Persuasion*. This book goes into detail using studies from social science and behavioral psychology, as well as evidence-based research to explain the psychology of why people say "yes."

Here is a definition of the C/C Principle,

"It is quite simply, our nearly obsessive desire to be (and to appear) consistent with what we have already done. And once we have made a choice or taken a stand, we will encounter personal and interpersonal pressures to behave consistently with that commitment. And those pressures will cause us to respond in ways that justify our earlier decision."

In summary, once we make a choice, we will obey personal and interpersonal pressures to behave consistently with that commitment.

This is best illustrated with one of the experiments that Cialdini describes in his book. In the 1980s, scientists undertook an experiment where they involved homeowners from a part of the city that had a high frequency of car accidents. They asked these homeowners to put up a big sign which said, "Drive Carefully" in front of their lawns. The result? Twenty percent of homeowners agreed. This was the control group.

Then there was a second group, and in this experiment they asked this group for an extra action a few weeks earlier. They had gone to the homeowners and asked to put a tiny sticker sign that read "Drive Carefully" on their fence. A few weeks later, they made the same request as to the first group, asking if they would mind putting up a big sign on their front lawn saying, "Drive Carefully."

What do you think was the difference in response between the two groups? Remember there was only one small difference between them. One group had been asked for such a tiny commitment earlier on that no one could refuse.

The results were this: 75% of the second group agreed to the big sign. *Seventy-five percent!* Three out of four of those asked agreed to put a huge sign disturbing the elegance of their front lawn, compared to 20% of the control group. Purely because of the C/C Principle.

Most of the second group agreed to put up the huge sign in order to be consistent with their earlier commitment. And the best thing about this experiment? Their earlier commitment was so tiny, so small, that it was guaranteed to get a yes. That's the power of the C/C Principle.

Salespeople understand this. It's widely known in sales psychology that once you get someone to say yes six times, your chances of making a sale go dramatically up. Very often you'll hear salespeople asking you simple "yes" questions like, "Are you looking to solve this XYZ problem?" or, "Is this XYZ benefit important for you?" Questions which are likely to elicit a positive response. As you start saying yes, your chances of agreeing to purchase the product go up.

So what does this mean for you? Well, let's look at how Ordinary Joe and Extraordinary Jennifer go about securing a promotion from their boss.

Ordinary Joe

Joe doesn't prep his boss through email about what the topic of the conversation will be. Instead he stops him in the corridor and initiates an important career conversation.

"Hi boss" (imagine any name instead of the word 'boss', it really doesn't matter).

" How can I help you, Joe?"

"Ah, well boss, I was thinking, I've been in this role for two years and a part of this organization for four years. I think it's time for me to move on to the next challenge. I'd like to discuss my next steps."

"That's great, Joe, that you're looking ahead in your career. Tell me, why should I promote you?"

At this point Joe is a little confused. He'd just given his reasons for being promoted. He has been a loyal employee for the past few years, and he deserves a promotion in exchange for his loyalty.

Joe becomes defensive and frustrated. I won't play out the rest of the conversation because I'm sure you can imagine how it ends. Joe becomes passive aggressive, his boss can't find a reasonable reason to promote Joe and gives him a "thanks, but no thanks" response.

Joe doesn't get a promotion, and remains trapped in his job title for years to come.

Now, shall we see how Jennifer handles the same situation?

Extraordinary Jennifer

First, Extraordinary Jennifer asks for a meeting request via email. She makes it clear that it's about her career development plan. It's a small ask and her boss agrees. Subconsciously her boss doesn't know it, but he's made a micro-commitment to her career development. It's the first step using the C/C Principle.

"Hi boss."

"Hey Jennifer. How can I help you?"

"Hi, as I mentioned in my email," (notice how she builds a bridge) "I wanted to talk with you about my career development plan. I want to know how I can best help you and the organization achieve their goals and also get a decent shot at advancing my career."

"Certainly Jennifer, what exactly are you thinking...."

Jennifer and her boss have a discussion about both of their goals, her One Big Thing, her strengths, and what the organization needs. She is ready for this conversation, she has clarity on who she is; she starts first by asking how she can help and only afterwards discusses her aspirations. At the end, she asks if what was talked about can be put in written form, and when is the best time to meet and finalize the conversation. These are a series of micro-commitments that get her boss invested in her success.. At the end her boss tells her this,

"Alright Jennifer. Why don't you put in writing what we just discussed as your career development plan and let me review it."

After reviewing the document, her boss takes the time out to think about what he wants Jennifer to achieve in a certain time frame and what her career path could look like. Now he is the one thinking and working on her career advancement!

Her boss made a commitment to discuss career development, and in order to be consistent with this decision, he is now working on her career advancement. This would never have happened if Jennifer had asked outright via email for her boss to think and work on it.

Here's a quote from an actual manager I asked about this approach,

"If you come to me as my subordinate and ask for me to lay out an xyz plan for you to achieve xyz, I take a great deal of time and

energy to lay out what could be expected by that date. I put it in writing, I give them a copy, I keep a copy, and I put a copy in their file. I also set a date to review the issue. When the date comes, I sit the person down and ask them to do a review on their performance."

So there you go, the C/C Principle in action. You ask your boss for a small commitment, a career development plan, and then in order to remain consistent with this commitment, he agrees to a performance review. Because the document is in writing, if you achieve the targets and goals he sets, he'll agree to promote you. Why? Because of the C/C Principle. He has an obsessive desire to be consistent with his earlier commitments.

If you want more strategies on how to manage your boss, get the free "cheat sheet" I've created for you: www.career10x.com/bonuses.

To Summarize:

- Extraordinary people don't climb to the top, but are carried there by the people they work with. In other words, in order to get promoted, you need your boss.
- The goal isn't to make your boss your ally, but to get them *working for you.*
- You can do this by understanding the four principles, seeing the world through their eyes, adjusting your style and using the C/C Principle to get them committed to your promotion.

Now that you know how to get your boss to work for you, it's time to find the secret weapon of the 10%. You'll learn how to *grow* into your next job title, instead of *getting* your next job title.

Chapter 8

You 2.0

There's a fundamental difference between how the 10% and the 90% approach their next role. It's the difference between *getting* your next job and *growing* into your next job. And in this chapter you'll learn how to do the latter.

If you remember, the Career Acceleration Formula looks like this:

Career Acceleration = Mindset x Value x Leverage

The last chapter, *"Make Your Boss Work For You,"* was dedicated to the first part of the final element of the formula: Leverage. Here, you're going to learn the second method to gaining leverage in your career.

A DREAM JOB WHILE GOING THROUGH AN MBA

While most students sit in lectures, taking notes on their laptops (which is usually already available on the college's Intranet), or are distracting themselves with social media or shopping on Amazon, Christina was busy arranging and coordinating her organization's activities in Spain via email and instant messenger. Christina had landed her dream position while doing her MBA. Most people usually choose to drop one or the other, but not Christina. She was now part of the 10% club, and she chose to do what most other people wouldn't, she chose to do both.

But just who is this superwoman? Well, let's back up a bit.

Christina has an unusual story, quite different from most of the people in my course. I originally designed Career Acceleration Formula to help people *who were already employed* enter the career fast track and get promoted. But, as you found out from Mark's story back in Chapter 4, it can also be used to accelerate your job search.

However, while Mark used the mindset of the 10% to ask the correct questions to position himself as the top candidate, Christina did something with this course that even I didn't think was possible.

Christina viewed getting her next job as a promotion. She used the formula, and especially this section about how to grow into her dream job, straight from unemployment, all while doing her MBA.

Christina had had a fairly successful career. Graduating with a degree in chemical engineering, she transitioned to a career in sales, working with a variety of companies in her home country of Greece. However, after a few years of going up the ladder in both the telecommunications and the shipping industries, Christina was burned out. She explains,

"I felt disappointed in the sense that I didn't have the opportunity to use all of my strengths in my latest job. I also intensively felt the need to do something... different. Something that would make a difference and would radically change my daily life."

Christina was disappointed with her latest job as a Key Account Manager in the telemarketing and hotel industry. She felt like she wasn't fulfilling her potential. From the outside, Christina appeared successful, but on the inside she was discontent with her current career.

It Was Time For A Change

Furthermore, there was another problem. At that particular moment, to say Greece's economic situation wasn't great would be an understatement. You would only needed to pick up a newspaper and flip to the global affairs section to see a new headline about Greece's economy. At the time when Christina was thinking of leaving, Greece had an unemployment rate of about 30%.

Many people in the 90% crowd would have been shocked by Christina for even thinking about leaving her job. *"You want to quit your job? Don't you understand just how lucky you are to have a job? Why would you want to quit?!"*

But Christina knew it was time for a change. She wanted to grow professionally and personally, and for that she'd decided a new job that challenged her was the way to go.

One day Christina had had enough, she sat down, took out a piece of paper and started to ask herself some big questions. She started to think about what she'd achieved in her career, thinking about where she was now, and where she wanted to be in the future. She asked herself, *"Where do I want to be one year from now?"*

The fact of the matter was Christina intensively felt the need to do something different in her life. She felt the need to do something that would make an impact, that would put a dent in the universe, and would entirely and radically change her life.

Not only in a bigger sense, but also that would change her daily life. Christina had a strong sense of her personal value, and she felt her current job was beneath that.

Realizing that the risk wasn't in leaving her job but in not making a change, Christina left her job and took a month off to relax.

After gaining some clarity, she decided to enroll in an MBA program. Her plan was to use the year to work out what she wanted to do, and by the end of her year, she'd have changed everything in her career.

One month into her MBA program she heard about my course, Career Acceleration Formula, and enrolled in the program.

Here is what she experienced:

"After the first few lectures of the course, my mindset switched. I started treating myself as the ultimate project in the job search market."

Christina instantly identified with the course, she loved the strategic nature of it, and she immediately started taking action.

She fully embraced the mindset of viewing herself as a product. She saw herself as a potential premium product, and did everything to get there.

She made a serious meeting with herself where she answered the questions of where she was and where she wanted to go, and she set about finding her competencies and strengths.

Like any manager in charge of a product, she did extensive research on the market. She looked deeply into the industries that she wanted to get into, with the goal of finding an industry and company that was a perfect fit for her.

After creating a mind map of herself and the companies she'd found that she loved, she started eliminating companies that didn't fit with her wants. She crossed them all off until she found one that was perfect for her.

However, this is where Christina really shines, she fully embraced the mindset of the 10%.

"Best people don't apply for best jobs, they create them."

Christina already viewed herself as a product, and she knew that she was the best product and it was time for her to sell herself in the best possible way.

Why is this important? Because of Greece's economic climate. When a country has an unemployment rate of 30%, everyone suddenly enters scarcity mode. People believe there are a limited amount of opportunities, so instead of setting out to create their dream job, everyone goes about responding to any job advert they can find, spamming anyone who has an electronic mailbox with their resumes.

This is why the 90% crowd remain in the 90%.

Christina, on the other hand, adopted a strategic approach that I talked about in my course. She identified five possible people she could contact inside her desired company. Most of them were potential warm contacts, people she could get an introduction to, but one of them was a cold contact. It was her backup, and it was surprisingly the only person who responded.

She then field tested her resume by sending it to a top company. When she got a call back, she knew her resume was in good shape.

Christina then used the mindset of *growing* into her next job, instead of getting her next job. She applied for an open position at the company just so she could meet the HR Director. Think about that for just a second. Her plan was to get a foot in the door by meeting the HR Director and then change the direction of the interview to propose the job that she really wanted!

Talk about courage.

Maybe... maybe some people in the 90% crowd would have gone as far as analyzing and working out what their dream job would be, but would quit when they realized there were no open positions in that role at the company they wanted.

But not Christina.

At the end of her interview the HR Director admitted, "You know... you're very good, and I have a more challenging proposal for you." As the HR Director started explaining the job role, Christina sat up and before she knew it she had accepted the offer. It was the perfect role.

After a series of challenging interviews with the CEO and President of the company, she landed her dream role, International Business Coordinator, overseeing five business operations in five countries.

This is how the hidden job market that we mentioned in Chapter 1 works, and you're going to find out how to tap into it.

Lessons Learned

When I asked Christina if there were any lessons she'd learned from the process, and she shared three:

Change Your Outlook On The Professional World

The course and her experience had given her a profound insight into how things really work in the professional world. She knew the power of the hidden job market, and the power of giving value first and solving problems.

No One Will Make The Job For You

I covered this in Chapter 4 and it's true. No one will make your dream job for you beforehand. You have to create your own opportunities and make a strategic plan to influence other people to help you achieve your goals. And when you hit setbacks, you shouldn't change your goal, you should change your plan and adapt.

Your True Competitor Is You

"Our actual competition is the ignorance of our uniqueness."
- Christina

It's very easy to view others as our competition, but this isn't the case. Everyone is unique; we all have unique strengths, and unique experiences that can give us an edge in a situation. But most of the time we're unaware of what makes us unique, and this is what can harm us in our career.

Christina was a busy bee when I talked to her. She worked full time and left two times a week to go to her afternoon lectures for her MBA. During these lectures, she would takes her laptop and all her tools and work in the background. She said it was tough, but she loved it. It was her dream job and she wouldn't have had it any other way.

GETTING VS. GROWING INTO YOUR NEXT JOB TITLE

If you do a search on Amazon or go on Google and search, how to get promoted, most of the blog and book titles you'll find will be something along the lines of, *"Get Your Next Job in 90 Days"* or *"How to Land The Job Of Your Dreams"*. However there is something fundamentally wrong in this approach. Words like "get" and "land" remind me of the hustler who is always looking to get what he wants, always grabbing, always seeking how to serve himself. People like that don't get far in the world; we use terms such as "moocher" or "leech" to describe them.

Think about it, do you want to be a leech?

By purchasing this book you have committed to being in the 10% club of people when it comes to your career acceleration. You're going to learn all the different processes where you *grow* into your next job. It's all about the mindset we talked about in Chapter 4; you have to give first before you can receive. You have to provide value upfront before you can get what you want.

Being like Ordinary Joe, who believes he is entitled to a promotion, is like a famous analogy Earl Nightingale used to use often, *"It's like the man who stands in front of the stove and says to it 'Give me heat and then I'll add the wood.'"* If you're like that man, you'll be waiting forever for the stove to light, and remain shivering and cold.

If you want to enter the career fast track, you have to give value up front.

I want you to stop for a moment and think about the people you know who are successful, the people who are in the 10% club, who are just promoted time after time, get unimaginable pay rises and all the perks. Come up with a specific name you know and think about that person. Have you noticed anything about them? Have you noticed that it isn't a matter of them landing job after job promotion, but that they grow so fast in their current job, that it becomes *natural* for them to move to the next job?

If you did, good, because that is *precisely* what happens. People in the 10% club grow so fast both personally and professionally that they become ready for their next job while still in their current job. Looked at that way, their promotion is a foregone conclusion.

They don't *pursue* and land their next job title. They pursue professional growth and their next job title comes to them as a result. That's the difference between getting a job title and growing into your next job title.

Consider the Hermit crab. This crab doesn't have a shell of its own; instead it wanders the seafloor looking for a discarded shell to make it its own. Throughout its life, the Hermit crab changes its shell a number of times. However it only gets a bigger shell when *it grows big enough* for a bigger shell. It doesn't try and look for a bigger shell when it isn't large enough, as it'll just be too unwieldy for it to use.

The same is true in your career. You don't get promoted until you've *grown* enough to fit into your next job title. Once you understand and use this principle, you'll be in the 10%. You'll have understood something that is so powerful, that you can get promoted whenever you want.

Why? Because if you only get a promotion once you've *grown* into the role, then it's simple. In order to get a promotion you have to grow, not chase and land a promotion. And growing is something that is completely under your control. Growing professionally and personally is something you can take the time out to do.

And you're going to learn some fast ninja tactics on how to do this.

Growing Means You Can
Access The Hidden Job Market

By using this approach of *growing* into your next job, you'll also unlock access to the hidden job market. I've talked about the hidden job market earlier on, but the concept is simple. Seven out of 10 jobs aren't announced or revealed. They are often only available via invitation, personal connections or the role is created for the candidate. However, 90% of people believe that job adverts are the only way to get a job. So you have 90% of people applying for three out of 10 jobs. That's a crowded marketplace.

So how do you get those hidden seven out of 10 jobs? Well, notice one of the criteria I mentioned before, *the role is created for the candidate.* Jobs in the hidden market are usually created for individuals who can solve a certain problem for the organization. Often a problem the organization didn't even know they had.

This is why the competition is so high for any job that's advertised, even if the pay is crap, and the job is boring.

I like to use the following visual representation to illustrate the hidden job market:

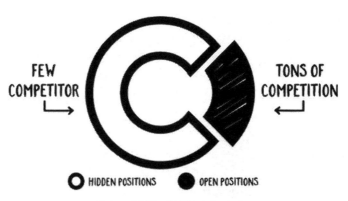

Figure 14: *The hidden job market*

Think about this for a second. Would you like to compete in the small pond that all the tourists are going to, to compete for the small 30% piece of the pie that everyone else applies for? Or would you like to play around in a huge sea, full of empty space, where there are fewer competitors? This is the difference between open positions and the hidden job market.

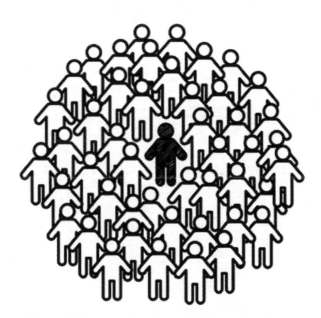

Figure 15: *Do you want to be one in the sea of applicants or the few that don't have to apply for their dream roles*

Think about this for a second. Would you like to compete in the small pond that all the tourists are going to, to compete for the small 30% piece of the pie that everyone else applies for? Or would you like to play around in a huge sea, full of empty space, where there are fewer competitors? This is the difference between open positions and the hidden job market.

So let's summarize. By following traditional career advice, you're not only missing out on 70% of available jobs out there, but you're competing with 90% of job candidates for 30% of the jobs.

If you've ever learned about business strategy, you'll probably have learned of red ocean vs. blue ocean strategy. The concept is simple, in business when competition is fierce it becomes like a red ocean, full of sharks bleeding while they fight each other over a limited amount of fish. Blue ocean strategy is simple, when the competition gets fierce, you should move to a new market where there is little competition and the fish are plentiful.

Following traditional career advice is the red ocean strategy, but accessing the hidden job market is the blue ocean strategy. You want to go to where there is less competition. You'll be ensuring that jobs are *created* for you as you grow into the role. If a job role is created for you and your strengths, then it is understood that you'll get the job. Your only competition is yourself.

As you learned from Christina's story, if you follow the strategy of this course, if you determine your next job title as I suggest in Chapter 5, then it becomes a lot easier to access the hidden job market. Christina knew the competencies of the role that she wanted, and she adopted a strategy of diverting the interview to talk about the role she really wanted, about the problem she wanted to solve for the organization.

But once you know your next job title, how can you grow into it? What strategies and tactics *can you* employ to get there?

I'm glad you asked. Let's find out the first thing you can do to grow into your job title.

TAKE THE 360 DEGREE VIEW

Something we do every day is we look in the mirror. We look in the mirror just before we go out to make sure our appearance is satisfactory to us. Why? Because we want to be at our best in front of others.

However, mirrors have a limitation. They only allow us to see our front. It's very hard to look at your back in the mirror, unless you have a room specially designed to do so. This isn't good because half the time people see our backs. Yet, we don't know what we look like from behind. This is a blind spot.

Similarly, doing a self-analysis of your strengths and weaknesses is like looking in the mirror. You only get half the story. In assessing yourself you have a blind spot, you don't know what others think of your competencies and your limitations.

This is where the 360 Degree Feedback comes in. If you've heard of the 360 Degree Feedback, then you know what I'm talking about. But keep reading because you'll also learn one or two nuggets that will allow you to use this feedback to nail your next job promotion.

The 360 Degree Feedback is a process in which employees receive confidential, anonymous feedback from the people that work around them. It typically involves the employee's immediate peers, managers, and people that directly report to them. In this sense, it gives a 360 degree view of your strengths and limitations from all the people around you.

The 360 Degree Feedback is heavily used in business. It's used by 90% of the companies in the Fortune 500, but is also extremely popular amongst small and medium businesses. Why? Because it's one of the most accurate ways to get professional feedback. There are 50 to 80 questions, and they take quantitative as well as qualitative feedback on your behaviors, your competence at work, and how you tackle challenges.

The last time I did a 360 Degree Feedback survey I came across a lot of hidden gems in the written insight my peers shared. For example, I was rated as having strong communication and influence skills, being very strategic and structured in my thinking, great at learning new ideas, and highly analytical. However my strongest weakness was my impatience, which resulted in some of my team members feeling insufficient and alienated. This was an eye opener. I learned that I needed to be more patient when interacting with others on my team, and not expect other people to move at my pace.

But the 360 Degree Feedback isn't only good at finding out where you stand among your colleagues, it's also good at calling out the elephant in the room.

For example, one of my students, Nick, was quite successful in his career. He had gotten promoted often and seemed to be on the career fast track. He came to me for coaching on how to get to his next role, as it was a bit of a challenge for him. I got Nick to do The Boss Test from my course and he believed his boss was supportive of him, but not active. Not a bad place to be, as you need your boss to work for you in order to get promoted. However I insisted he carry out a 360 Degree Feedback survey, and then to come to me afterwards so we could analyze the results together.

And that's when we discovered something surprising. The feedback coming from his boss and from his peers was completely different, and it was clear that despite what Nick thought, his boss wasn't that supportive of him in his career. Nick was at first disappointed with these results, but then he got over it. And this was great, because we could now craft an action plan to get his boss to be more supportive of him, allowing him to get the job promotion he wanted.

By just making one simple survey, Nick was able to save himself a potential year of heartache, working hard on his promotion believing his boss was on his side, only for it to all fall apart at the end. As I said before, you *need* your boss to be supportive of you in order to get promoted. You can't do it without them.

Better to get an accurate measure of where you stand professionally among your colleagues and your boss than to make guesses.

Additionally, this survey is important as it'll allow you to identify skills and competencies that are required for your next role that you don't have now. This gives you the time to start improving in these areas so that there are no objections when it comes to you getting promoted. It also will make you more effective in your new position.

Finally, taking a 360 Degree Feedback survey will make you stand out. It signals to your colleagues and to your boss that you are serious about your career. You're essentially saying, "I'm dedicated to personal growth and getting promoted." It's a great way to make people take notice of you.

Think about it; imagine you were the coach, or even the president of a professional sports team. When it comes to investing time and resources in one of your players, which player are you more likely to help out? The one that comes to you often and asks *"Coach, can you check me out on the field, and point out anything I can improve upon?"* Or the one that never comes asking for feedback, and believes they have an accurate measure of his performance?

Of course you'll choose the former. They're signaling to you that they're serious about improving their ability and performance, and that they're a worthy investment. It's the same with asking for a 360 Degree Feedback survey.

GET CLARITY ON YOU 2.0

Figure 15: Point A: Where You Are. Point B: Where You Want To Go

It's time for you to get clear on your "You 2.0." What is this? Well your "You 2.0" is the end point of your journey. It's the crystal clear destination of where you're heading on this career journey. But it isn't just your job title; it's the set of skills and behaviors that you're going to need to be ready for your next role. Remember, we're growing into your next job role, not just getting it. Why? Because the crowd is crowded and they are going for the 30% of open job positions.

But by being clear on your "You 2.0," you'll be able to play in the hidden job market, you'll be able to grow into the perfect job role that lies in the 70% job market that isn't open.

From Chapter 5 you've already identified your perfect next job title, and this is closely linked with this process.

What the 90% do when it comes to looking for their next job title is they are always looking for something "better" than their current job title. Always searching on job boards for something that is a little better than what they currently have going on, whether it's the job title or the company. And they never make progress.

Ordinary Joe in the 90% crowd doesn't have any awareness of where he's starting out. He doesn't know what he's strongest at in his skills and behaviors, he doesn't know how others perceive him, and he doesn't know his point B. He doesn't know the destination that will best use his natural talents so he can have an amazing career. He has absolutely no clarity on where he is, or where he is going. And that's why he's destined to fail.

> *"If one does not know to which port one is sailing, no wind is favorable."*
> - Seneca

This is why it's easy for HR to keep Ordinary Joe happy. He's easy to manage and not expensive to keep. You give him a 2% pay raise every year, and he'll stay at his one job for a long time. Perfect for the organization, as many Joes can occupy all the lower roles of the job pyramid.

But where do the 10% differ? How does Extraordinary Jennifer differ from Ordinary Joe?

- She takes time to get clarity on her strengths, her competitive advantage and the right environment for her to thrive (See Chapter 5).
- She asks herself what the perfect job would be for her, both in the short term and the long term.
- Following the 360 Degree Feedback, she then builds the skills and competencies required for the job. She also builds the influence required to grow into that job role, which we'll talk about in the next chapter.

This means Jennifer has clarity on where she's starting from, Point A, and also Point B, which is her next job title and what is needed for her to get there. HR works hard to keep Jennifer because upper management keeps asking them, "What are you doing to retain our top talent," which is why they offer her hefty incentives to stay and promote her often. She gets all the bonuses, top training programs, and access to top mentors in the organization.

CHOOSE YOUR SIMULATION PROJECT

The final part of growing into your "You 2.0" is in choosing your simulation project.

Now just what do I mean by a simulation project? What is it for, and just what exactly is it?

Well, first let's define your simulation project. It's a project or a piece of work that you volunteer to lead and will, in return, generate undeniable proof for your next employer that you're ready for your next job.

Why is this necessary? Why do you need a project that you volunteered to lead in order to show your boss that you're ready for a promotion?

Think about the mindset of your future boss, who is basically the hiring manager of your next job. Your future boss cares about two things. First, she wants to ensure that you are the right person who can get the job done. She doesn't really care what or where you got the experience for the job, all she cares is finding someone who is really good and has undeniable proof that they can do what's required.

Even so, while your future boss doesn't really care where you got the experience, she still has to follow the rules and the process of

190

the organization. She has to get someone who has the *right* experience so that she can tick the boxes that come from HR, who demand that the system be followed. But really at the end of the day, all your future boss cares about is that you can get the job done.

Your future boss's worst nightmare is simple, they hire someone who isn't capable of doing the job. Not only because the job doesn't get done, but because it makes them look bad to the organization, thus hurting *their* career. Your future boss wants to hire someone who can do the job so well, that the project becomes a beacon to the organization. Why? Because if you do the job well, it makes her look good, and *she* becomes more successful. This is a critical piece of psychology to understand. Your simulation project isn't about you; it's about your future boss.

Yet, this is where we get a Catch 22 situation. When in an interview you get asked, "So what experience do you have with X," where X is something related to your future job title, the candidate thinks, "Just how the hell am I going to have the experience if I don't yet have a job that offers me that experience?" And this Catch 22 is where most people stop and give up on the career ladder.

Second, your future boss is worried about your competence. How can you prove to him that you're competent enough for the next job if you've never been in such a job? How does he know you won't crack under the pressure?

Sometimes the way to interrupt your thinking to solve a thorny problem such as this is to ask yourself an extraordinary question.

Back when I was trying to figure out how to get out of this conundrum, I stopped and asked myself a weird, but profound question that changed everything.

It's pretty simple.

"How does a country's government ensure that a $150 Million combat aircraft isn't destroyed by an incompetent pilot?"

Let's look at a popular fighter aircraft. The F-22 Raptor is a single seat, twin engine, all-weather stealth tactical aircraft developed and flown by the United States Air Force. The R&D program to develop the aircraft cost the U.S government $67 Billion. Each aircraft cost the government $150 Million.

This is not a cheap tool.

Clearly, with such an expensive aircraft, the last thing you want is an incompetent pilot, or someone who is mentally unhinged to fly and crash the aircraft. If they did so, you just flushed $150 Million down the drain. So how do they prevent this scenario?

Well, first the Air Force does something quite simple; they give potential pilots smaller and cheaper airplanes to fly. These trainer jet aircraft cost about a few million dollars. So if someone destroys these aircraft because of their incompetence, it only costs the government a few million dollars, and not *$150 Million*.

Then the Air Force also makes heavy use of computer simulators. These simulators look just like the real aircraft, but are instead running the software that imitates the real thing. Inside this simulator it looks just like a video game. And like in a video game, there is no risk. However the pilot operates the simulator just like a real aircraft, executing missions and flight maneuvers, and the Air Force measures their performance. This allows the pilot to not only improve his skill at little risk, but also to demonstrate to the Air Force that he has what it takes to fly their expensive $150 Million F-22 Raptor.

And this is what I mean by a simulation project in your career. In order to minimize the worries of your future boss, you should volunteer to lead a project that "simulates" your future job. You not only demonstrate that you're serious and want the job by volunteering to lead, but it's a chance for your future boss to see you in action, to see that you're competent enough for the next job title.

It also allows you to avoid the Catch 22 scenario, and you are able to get the necessary experience for the next job.

How does a freelancer land a new gig, or an artist get a new commission? They have a portfolio of work that demonstrates to the potential client that they're competent enough to undertake the work. It's why most advice out there for new artists or freelancers is they should volunteer to do a project for free or for cheap, to show future patrons that they have what it takes to get the job done.

I'll give you a more relatable example of how one person used a simulation project to get ahead in their career.

Ryan Graves, one time CEO now currently the head of global operations for Uber, has been estimated to be worth $1 Billion. But it wasn't always so glamorous for him.

In 2008, Ryan Graves had a dead-end job as a database administrator for GE Healthcare. It was an uninspiring job that was crushing his soul. In mid-2009, Ryan decided to make a radical change.

At the time, he was a fan of an up-and-coming startup called Foursquare, an app that allows people to check in on their mobile phones, while rating and reviewing business establishments. Ryan decided this was the job for him.

For this reason, he did what anyone who wants to work at a certain company would do, he submitted a job application, but was turned down.

Ryan wasn't deterred. Realizing he wasn't hired because he didn't have the competencies for the job, he decided to run a simulation project of his own. Ryan decided to *pretend* to work for Foursquare. He cold called bars around his home in Chicago, explaining the benefits of the app, and showing them how it worked, encouraging them to sign up. After some time, he was able to sign up 30 customers to the app.

Ryan then emailed this list of new customers to people connected with Foursquare, including their investors. He was promptly brought on board to help with their business development.

Later on he used his smarts to become Uber's first employee and is consequently now worth $1 Billion.

The simulation project was key for Ryan. He didn't even volunteer, but pretended to work at Foursquare and signed up 30 customers. When he sent the results of his work to his future bosses, he proved he had the competencies and the experience required for the job he wanted.

The 90% believe that volunteering to lead a job is a waste of time and opens themselves up to risk. The 10% know that volunteering to lead a project minimizes the risk for their future employers, and is the ninja tactic to display to their future bosses that they have what it takes to get the job done.

Choose a simulation project, and you'll grow into that next job role faster than you ever thought possible.
If you want to find out how I use simulation projects, I've outlined how I got promoted by volunteering to lead a proposal put forth by my organization. I've also created a checklist to help you identify the correct simulation project for your next job title. You can get both at: www.career10x.com/bonuses.

To Summarize:

- The 90% crowd view their promotion as getting their next job. The 10% club view a promotion as them growing into their next job title. This is how they access the hidden job market.
- A 360 Degree Feedback survey allows you to identify the strengths and competencies required for your next job title. It also signals to your peers and boss that you're serious about professional growth.
- Having clarity on your destination dramatically raises your chances of success, as you'll know the strengths and traits required for the next job title.
- Choosing a simulation project provides undeniable proof to your future boss that you'll do a good job and won't let her down. It also gets you out of the Catch 22 situation of not having any experience.

Now that you know how to grow into your next job title, it's time to learn the final tool to gain you leverage in your Promotion. It's time to become the center of influence in your organization.

"In two and a half months, I created MY OWN BRAND NEW PERFECT JOB, which didn't exist before and hadn't been announced to the public."
- Christina

Chapter 9

A BECOMING THE CENTER OF INFLUENCE

Welcome to the sixth and final element of the Career Acceleration Formula.

First of all, I want to congratulate you on making it this far. This is proof that you're serious about taking your career and paycheck to the next level.

This final element is the secret sauce to truly leveraging your skills to get onto the career fast track. Let's recall:

Career Acceleration = Mindset x Value x Leverage.

I can tell you from my experience and the experience of my students that becoming the center of influence in your organization is the Archimedes lever that will accelerate your career. Once you have influence, even if you haven't nailed down the prerequisites (which you should), you will start to see phenomenal success in your career.

By becoming influential, you are focusing on the critical part of the "Leverage" part of the equation, and this allows you to multiply everything else. It allows your One Big Thing to become 10x more valuable to the organization. It allows you to grow faster into You 2.0. It ensures that your boss starts working for you faster than he would have before. Influence, to put it simply, is the most important skill you can learn to multiply your efforts to get you into the 10% club.

I had to dedicate an entire chapter to influence because it is the most important skill you can learn for success. Period. Whether it's growing your influence in the workplace or becoming the go-to person if you move to a new organization. Whether you want to recruit the right people as an entrepreneur or attract donors in a non-profit, influence will be the number one skill you'll use to achieve all these goals.

Don't believe me? Let's see how Dylan, a student of mine, used influence to go from zero to hero in his organization...

ENTER DYLAN

A few months ago, before Dylan hired a career coach and purchased my course, he was what I would call an "anonymous cog" in his organization. He'd been trapped in his role for seven years and was frustrated with his job. If you'd asked his manager's colleagues for Dylan they'd have given you a questioning glance, "Dylan who?"

Compare this with today's state of affairs. Dylan is a person of influence in his organization and is known outside his immediate circle. His Inbox is full of meeting requests and his contact list is packed with the names of other influential people in his organization. Oh, and he's been promoted to a new job title and got a substantial raise, to boot.

But how did Dylan get here? How did he become so influential in a matter of months? To explain that we have to look at the background of his story.

While Dylan has a Psychology undergraduate degree, he's mostly been in the technology sector. With his MBA, he became a Senior Project Manager in an engineering organization that works with a global financial services provider. He'd been in this role for seven years and while he occupied a niche no one else did, he was frustrated.

Why?

Because while the organization had made great strides forward while he was there, and had grown from handling business on a local level to a global level, Dylan hadn't seen a change in his job title.

He had been trapped in his role, despite seven years of growth in the organization, and he was frustrated. Though he had received the standard annual salary raise, he wanted a higher degree of acknowledgement from his organization. He wanted to be recognized for the value he brought to the table.

Dylan had a realization:

"I knew I needed to do something different if I was going to get a different result. There was a reason I wasn't being promoted. No one had it out for me, so I knew it was something I was doing or not doing. Something I was being or not being. I had to go and learn to do or not do something. To be or not to be something different."

As a result of this realization, Dylan attended the Landmark Forum, a three-day course, and his eyes were further opened. His long held beliefs were challenged, and he left with a deeper realization that he was responsible for everything in his life.

Understanding this, he started to take action. While I don't normally recommend this, Dylan hired a career coach and started assessing what was possible and available in his career.

Before Dylan came across my course, his career coach got him to do something quite valuable.

"Look, you've been there for seven years, you must have done SOMETHING useful if you've been thinking about growing your career?"

"Yeah... I guess."

"Let's make a list of the things you've done that were significant, that made a difference."

Dylan sat down and made such a list. His coach then got him to assign a dollar value to each of his achievements. What was the cost saving or revenue generated for such activities to the organization. Dylan did the math and was able to identify millions of dollars that he had contributed to his organization. This was a real eye opener and made him realize how valuable he was to his organization.

Around this time, Dylan came across my course and realized that he could take what he learned from his coach and multiply his results with my course, by knowing <u>exactly</u> who to connect with and what <u>exactly</u> to say. Dylan had contributed millions of dollars to his organization, but the problem was that no one knew who he was. If they didn't know him, how could they acknowledge his contribution?

He started to evaluate how close he was to his manager and other managers in the organization. He then assigned himself some homework. He started making half an hour "Getting To Know You" conversations with people in his organization. From there he could pivot to talk about his achievements.

But how did he go about this?

Becoming Influential

In September, Dylan started pitching his boss and other managers an email along these lines, *"Hey, here's what I've done for our organization. This is how we can work together to do more to contribute towards your goals."*

He also tailored his email to be person-specific. If it was appropriate, he would list specific accomplishments which fell under the umbrella of that manager's responsibilities.

Once he did this, Dylan started being invited to meetings and doors started to open. While talking to a colleague or a manager, he would focus on letting people know he wanted to do more and the way he could help them. He displayed his eagerness to grow and talked about where he wanted to go. Dylan's organization had a culture where this was encouraged; people were happy to share and talk about their goals.

As Dylan started going to these meetings, he started hearing about opportunities, but something magical also happened. During some of these meetings, the person he was talking to would suddenly realize another person Dylan could talk to. They'd then promise to refer Dylan their way.

This was brilliant as Dylan now had a warm introduction to people he couldn't have approached before. A cold email would have got a polite no, but now a recommendation from someone the person knows? He was sure to get a yes.

The results of these meetings snowballed, and Dylan became known not only by his boss, but his boss's peers, managers in global roles, and his boss's boss. Dylan came to be known by six to seven influential people in his organization, which meant whenever any future conversations came up regarding promotions in his area, his name would come up.

As a result of Dylan's influence, he was promoted within five months to a Program Manager, with extra responsibilities, a raise, and some perks.

But most importantly for Dylan, his organization now recognizes him. They recognize what he has to offer and are giving him more responsibility and extra challenges, allowing him to grow and prove what he's capable of.

When I asked Dylan if he had any lessons to share he had some insightful comments that I just had to write down.

Influence Is About Being Known

"Influence is really about being known. If you're known by the people who have conversations with the people above you, your name will come up. If you don't, then when they're talking about raises, bonuses and promotions, they can't say they know what you did, nor can they support you. They know who you are, and what your role is, but that's it. If you're unknown you don't get as many votes, and as a result, you're underrepresented."

I couldn't have said it better myself. Remember this strategy is about stacking the odds in your favor and giving yourself an unfair advantage. By having your name be top of mind among your future manager and anyone he's going to talk to about a promotion, you're more likely to receive support when you're not in the room. If, however, you're not known, then there is no one to present and support you. It's that simple.

Doing Isn't Enough, You Have To Show The Desire To Grow

"If you're successful in a role and a great doer, if you're happy to do the work and people love you, then management won't want to take you out of that role."

However, if you start displaying *the desire* to move upwards and to be granted extra responsibility, then suddenly the conversation changes.

"I could have done my job forever, but the minute I stuck my head up and said 'Hey, what else is possible?' it suddenly becomes a completely different conversation. But I had to start it. So don't let other people run your career, because they'll probably run it in a direction you don't want."

You Have To Make Yourself Known By Having Conversations

"Until you tell them you want to do something different, nothing will happen. But when you do, then they'll know, 'Oh, hey, we have this guy who wants to do something different. He's going to challenge himself and us. Let's see what we can have him do.'"

When I asked Dylan about his future he was ecstatic. He's ultimately excited about the recognition he's received from his organization, and has high hopes for the future. He knows he is responsible for the destiny of his career, and knows he can steer it in any direction he wants.

WHY INFLUENCE BEATS HIERARCHY

> *"Influence is the ability to get people to do what you want them to do, but for the reasons that they come up with themselves or for the reasons that they already have."*
> - Tony Robbins

Now let's look at your standard organization. You may believe that once someone becomes a manager that they are leaders, that they have influence in the organization, but that's simply not true in today's world. A manager simply instructs the people underneath her on what to do, and they follow those instructions. A leader however, inspires and influences *whomever* she wants in her organization, whether that person is above her, below her or is her peer, to move in the direction that she wants them to do.

That's the difference between influence and hierarchy. The person who has influence doesn't need formal power to lead, she simply leads and people follow, even if they're above her in the hierarchy.

When Brad Garlinghouse, a little-known senior manager, wrote a memo to his bosses at Yahoo in 2006 outlining what was wrong with the company and the direction they were going, it caused an uproar. The memo was leaked and the *Wall Street Journal* reprinted it. Traditional thinking is that this is career suicide - you shouldn't rock the boat and you <u>definitely</u> shouldn't tell your bosses what's wrong.

But here's the thing, when Brad Garlinghouse wrote that memo he was exercising *influence*. By talking about the hopes and fears of the organization, he was able to get senior management and the board at Yahoo to do what he wanted, but for the reasons they came up with themselves. The memo started a chain of events that led to the then CEO of Yahoo, Terry Semel's departure and some big changes at Yahoo.

Oh and guess what happened to Brad? He got promoted.

Could Brad have waited until he was CEO or VP, thereby having formal power and be able to instruct others to exercise upon his vision? Maybe, but then there's no guarantee that Brad would have reached that level. Instead he used *influence* to get Yahoo to make some serious changes.

That's the power of leading with influence rather than instruction. Your position doesn't matter.

What's At The Heart Of Office Politics?

Something I've realized is that many people mistake influence for office politics. They confuse the two, believing that the only way to gain influence is to engage in office politics.

I can see you already cringe; you're already hesitant because you hate the idea of office politics. And guess what, so do I! I absolutely hate it, and I'll show you why.

You might have heard this phrase often, *"Oh, I like working in my organization. It's huge, and has a lot of opportunities for my career. But I hate the office politics that goes with it."*

I bet that the person who said that has never really thought about what office politics really means. They've never thought about their workplace in terms of influence and relationships, but in terms of backstabbing and deception.

Let's get to the heart of what office politics is: It's engaging in what I call "CYA" activity. "CYA" stands for Cover Your Ass. It's a form of seeking certainty. Most of the 90%, in what they do at work every day, are trying to cover their ass. Whether it's how they phrase their emails, whether it's how they suggest ideas, the 90% is trying to cover their ass. Trying to make sure they're not "rocking the boat" or suggest something too provocative. They're worried about how others perceive them.

They're trying to seek certainty, making sure that they won't lose their jobs or make anyone dislike them.

This makes people engage in the following activities:

Truth Twisting

Something I've noticed over the years is that there are quite a few people out there who are gifted with language. They are powerful communicators and understand how to make things larger than life.

They're able to package and describe something that's actually crap, and make it sound amazing. Maybe they didn't really achieve anything that week, however after they've finished recounting what they got done that week, you'll find yourself nodding your head and excited at the forward momentum on the project. Yet, it's all empty air. They'll use buzzwords that make what they did appear larger than life and revolutionary. But at the end of the day, you'll probably find yourself picking up the slack later on because of their deception.

These people are also skilled at presenting and making something that's mundane appear extraordinary, and while this can be a useful skill in quite a few fields, it's horrible when it comes to office politics.

I call this "truth twisting." It's something I dislike in the workplace and it takes quite a bit of time to detect it. You have to develop a nose for it. Often it goes undetected and can lead to problems in the future.

Idea Stealing

This is straightforward. You've met quite a few people in the workplace who go around stealing ideas. Most often they'll be people you dislike, or bosses you don't get along with, as they will steal someone else's idea and reframe it as theirs. That's another manifestation of office politics.

Office Gossip

Gossip can seem quite harmless at first, talking about a coworker or a manager behind their back. It often surprises me how convinced people are that this gossip won't reach the subject of the conversation.

If you've ever played the telephone game as a child, you'll understand just how fast rumors can spread and get distorted through a social group. And that's without social media and instant messaging tools.

People who engage in office gossip are shooting themselves in the foot. It's going to reach the person you're talking about within the next hour, and most likely they'll know who it's from.

Back Stabbing

This is the worst form of office politics. We all know what it is, and it doesn't deserve any further comment.

I'm sure you understand that none of these activities are going to get you on the fast track to your perfect job. Managing your influence and your relationships, on the other hand, will. Let's compare the two.

How Extraordinary Jennifer Achieves Her Goals

When you look at the 10% club, the people in your organization and other organizations who have a lot of influence, you notice a few things. They don't engage in office politics, but they have a collection of behaviors in common.

Extraordinary Jennifer, a representative of this club, doesn't engage in certainty seeking activities, instead she takes educated risks. She doesn't just pull her ideas out of nowhere, trying to be interesting and innovative. Instead she is constantly doing her research, looking inside her industry for examples of new ideas, but also horizontally, looking for ideas in other industries that could work for her company. She sees what works and what doesn't, and then she comes up with an idea on which she's willing to take an educated risk.

What do I mean by an educated risk? I mean that Jennifer has done her research and strongly believes the idea will work, even though she understands there's a small chance that it won't. But doing the math, she's willing to back this idea 100%, and doesn't need to cover her ass. She isn't scared of rocking the boat, because she'll use her influence to recruit people to get on her side. Jennifer also doesn't try to cover her ass to keep her job, because she knows that being safe is risky. On the other hand, if she backs this idea and rocks the boat, she's counter-intuitively protecting her job. Even if the idea doesn't work, her reputation will increase as people respect that she went out on a limb for an idea.

Jennifer also presents her views as her views; she owns them 100%. She doesn't try and twist the language of her idea to seem less provocative, but stands behind it. This is powerful as it puts her in charge of her work and of her future.

Jennifer doesn't steal ideas; she does something radically different. When she takes someone else's idea, she talks about the person and praises them, making them the hero. This builds trust, gives value, and makes people more willing to help her, but it also uses the halo effect. By praising others, Jennifer intuitively knows that it'll come back to her. That people will associate her with people who have winning ideas.

In addition to that, Jennifer doesn't engage in office gossip or office backstabbing. First, because it's a waste of her time, and second, because it doesn't serve any purpose. Instead Jennifer is respectful of others, no matter their position, in every possible communication channel. Jennifer is a professional.

The final advantage Jennifer holds is that even though she doesn't have much formal power, she has influence throughout her organization. When she speaks, top management listens because she has a proven track record, and she goes out of her way to speak in a language they understand.

In fast moving organizations like Google and Facebook, formal power matters less and less. Divisions are formed into autonomous teams and are led by influential individuals, people who've gone out of their way to build up their influence and seduce everyone to their point of view. Seth Godin calls this building your "tribe." Influence ignores hierarchies, and the fastest growing startups know this.

THE 6 PRINCIPLES OF INFLUENCE

So how does influence work? How do these individuals have this skill that ignores hierarchies and is able to get others to do what they want, for the reasons they come up with themselves?

Well, in order to show you how certain influence strategies work on our psyche, I have to share an interesting story about mother turkeys.

In the relatively new science of ethology, which is the study of animals in their native settings, M.W. Fox discovered something about turkey mothers.

Usually turkeys are great mother's, loving, watchful, and protective of their young. They do what animal mothers do, tend and care for their young. However there is something odd about what makes them care for their young. It isn't the appearance of turkey chicks, or their smell, or touch. No, turkey mothers identify their young by the "cheep cheep" sound they emit. Once they hear this sound, turkey mothers enter mothering mode and care for their young.

So reliant are they on this sound that turkeys will even take in a polecat, the natural enemy of turkeys, if it makes this sound. Usually the appearance of a polecat triggers the turkey to squawk and peck in rage. Researchers found that even if a stuffed model polecat approaches a turkey, the same reaction occurs. But make that model stuffed turkey emit the "cheep cheep" noise of a turkey chick, and the turkey enters maternal mode. It will take the stuffed polecat under it and tend it like a turkey chick. Once the sound stops playing, the polecat receives a vicious attack.

Let that sink in for a second. The turkey will accept and care for a natural enemy just because it emits the sound of a turkey chick. It's almost as if there's an automatic program embedded in the turkey's psyche that makes it perform a certain action, a certain behavior.

Ethologists have found many instances of such behavior and that it is far from unique in only belonging to the turkey. Now, if you are thinking, *"Well Bozi, that's all well and fine for animals, but humans aren't stupid,"* I'll point you to the next study I'm about to share.

A well-known fact in psychology is that we'll be more successful in asking someone for a favor if we provide a reason. We simply like to have a reason to do something. However, Ellen Langer at Harvard showed something surprising in the following experiment.

First, she asked a small favor of people waiting in line to use a library copying machine, *"Excuse me, I have five pages. May I use the Xerox machine because I'm in a rush?"* The effectiveness of this request plus reason was astounding, 94% of those asked let her slip in front of the queue. When compared to when she just made the request, *"Excuse me, I have five pages. May I use the Xerox machine?"* only 60% agreed. That's the difference between nearly complete agreement and three out of five people agreeing.

Initially it's easy to conclude why the first request worked, *"It was because she was in a rush."* But Langer showed that not to be the case in the follow-up study.

Langer made another request, but instead of including a real reason to make people agree, she just included the word "because," and added no new information, just stating the obvious, *"Excuse me, I have five pages. May I use the Xerox machine because I have to make some copies?"* The results were again impressive, 93% of people she asked agreed.

This is powerful. Langer didn't include any new information, and her reason wasn't even a real one. She stated the obvious *"Can I make some copies, because I have to make some copies,"* yet people agreed anyway. It was almost like an automatic behavior was triggered in the people asked, simply because the word "because" was used.

You can find stories like this in Robert Cialdini's bestselling book, *Influence: The Psychology of Persuasion,* which illustrate the power of autonomic behaviors that are governed by your unconscious mind. These are behaviors that are outside of your conscious control, yet govern your day-to-day interactions.

Think about this, what do you do when you see someone smiling? You automatically smile back; you can't help yourself. It's an automatic reaction.

This is how influence works. They is a set of actions which trigger autonomic behaviors in others. Behaviors that are outside of their conscious control, but still govern their interactions. The key to being able to influence someone is to tap into a behavior governed by their unconscious. Their conscious minds will then make up reasons to justify why they're doing what they're doing.

This isn't the only component of being influential. Another part is being authentic. You have to be authentic, and be yourself, instead of being manipulative and deceptive about your actions. Why? Because you're not a robot, and people aren't robots. We can sense when someone is trying to manipulate us, and this leads to a break in trust. You may be able to influence them that one moment, but definitely not in the future.

So the six principles of influence, as shared by Robert Cialdini are as follows:

Reciprocation

This is simple, and it ties into the mindset I shared in Chapter 4 of *Value First*. When someone gives you something or does a favor for you, you're more likely to do what they ask.

This is why you're more likely to be received favorably by someone if you give them a gift up front. For example, when you welcome your new boss with a bottle of their favorite wine or a book you'll know they'll like, your boss will most likely reciprocate your kindness.

Consistency

We've talked about this principle in Chapter 7. This simply states that when we get someone to agree to a small favor first, we are more likely to get them to do a related big favor in the future, because they want to preserve the image they have of themselves. As human beings, we have a strong desire to remain consistent to our actions and beliefs, and when used correctly, this is a powerful tool of influence.

In the workplace, this principle is applied quite simply, always ask for one thing at a time. When you write an email, or have a meeting, ask for one small action at the end, not five.

Social Proof

This is my favorite and it's also pretty straightforward. Basically, the actions of others influence you, particularly when you're unsure of something. We are, for instance, more likely to become friends with someone who has quite a few friends, than with the person who has none.

Here's how to use social proof in the workplace. Imagine you have lunch with someone important in a highly visible location. For example, you're sitting with a VP at the central table in the company's restaurant. Imagine what happens when others look at this scenario. They'll start to talk about you. Suddenly you'll start generating huge social proof. You can do that. Also, you can use a testimonial from an important person or an influential customer. Marketers do this all the time. When did you last see a movie poster without a quote from an influential media outlet?

Likeability

This one is elementary and obvious, yet is often overlooked. When you like someone, you're more likely to do what they ask of you. However, I've often found people ignore this at work.

They believe results will talk more than their character. They concentrate on getting the message across, and not on basic manners. I'm not saying go out of your way to please everyone, that's what killed me in my second job, but just engage in simple etiquette. At work always be smiling, don't be a negative guy. Help others and have a generally good energy. Always be courteous and compliment others when you can. Be well dressed and groom yourself. Human beings are highly visual, so we place a great emphasis on how people present themselves.

There's a scene in the 2013 movie *Rush,* which portrays the infamous rivalry between James Hunt and Niki Lauda in Formula 1 racing during the 1970s. In 1976, before the Nuremberg race, the weather conditions were abysmal. The Nuremberg track was already notorious for causing a lot of accidents and fatalities. Niki Lauda held a meeting for the drivers just before the race and called for a vote to postpone the race.

His arguments were simple, the weather made the race more risky and this increased the chances of a horrible accident happening. However, James Hunt opposed Lauda, claiming that Niki was only calling for a postponement as it allowed him to secure his lead in the tables. When a vote was called, James won the vote, despite his lack of logical argument. Why? Because James was a very likeable guy, while Niki was arrogant and aloof. Niki didn't get his way because no one liked him.

The result of this became historic. Niki Lauda suffered a crash which left him covered with second and third degree burns for the rest of his life. Despite this, he continued to race and won three F1 World Championships in his career. However had he been able to sway the drivers to his point of view in that meeting he might have been able to reach the same achievements without suffering the consequences of the infamous crash.

Don't become likeable for vanity, do it because it matters. And when it comes to the time when you need to request a favor, people are more likely to agree. Why? Because they like you.

Authority

This principle of influence is huge. There are some professions which have authority built in, for example if you're in a hospital and you see someone in a lab coat and wearing a stethoscope, you immediately assume they're a doctor, and you'll defer to their authority. The same goes with a policeman; just the sight of him in uniform is enough to communicate authority.

Outside of those professions, there are more subtle ways to communicate authority. For example, getting an influential mentor on your side is a powerful way to communicate authority, or speaking on stage is another one. Being a clear communicator and always having facts to hand is also another way to communicate authority.

I'll give a brief example of how anyone can assume and communicate authority.

Back in 1977, there was an 18-year old busboy named Walter Bailey who worked at the Beverly Hills Supper Club, a popular nightclub and theatre near Cincinnati. Around 8.30pm on May 28, a fire started due to faulty wiring. Two waitresses walked into the room, took notice of the fire and alerted their supervisors. Fire trucks were immediately dispatched, but no effort was made to evacuate the club's customers. At the time of the fire, nearly 3,000 people were in the building. Because the building was old and lacked adequate firewalls, the blaze began to quickly spread to other parts of the club.

When the fire started, Bailey was working in another room, clearing dishes as over 1,000 people listened to a comedic act. A waitress told him about the fire, and he immediately let his supervisor know and recommend that he clear out the room. His supervisor just gave him the brush. What did this 18-year old busboy know about anything? Bailey was about to find the club owners when he stopped and thought to himself, *"This is stupid. I'm wasting time. Either he has to clear this room or I will."* He notified his supervisor again, but the man just shrugged and walked away. This was when Walter Bailey took matters into his own hands.

Before, no customer would have listened to an 18-year old busboy about anything, let alone the fact they had to evacuate a building. But Walter was smart. He boldly walked up the steps of the stage where the comedic act was happening and grabbed the microphone right from the hands of the performer. As an awkward silence fell over the crowd, he simply stated, *"I want everyone to look to my right. There is an exit in the right corner of the room. And look to my left. There's an exit to the left. And now look to the back. There's an exit in the back. I want everyone to leave the room calmly. There's a fire at the front of the building."* Then he left to warn other customers in other parts of the club.

The fire soon consumed the building and led to 165 fatalities, becoming the third worst fire disaster in the United States, but thanks to the actions of Walter Bailey, hundreds survived the fire that otherwise wouldn't have.

But what does this have to do with authority? Walter Bailey didn't have any authority to begin with; he was a lowly busboy. But by stepping up to the stage and grabbing the microphone, he instantly communicated authority. By calmly instructing people to evacuate because there was a fire, suddenly Walter was someone to listen to. He was a figure of authority telling people to evacuate the club.

Authority is subjective, learn how to communicate authority in the workplace, and you'll gain influence.

Scarcity

This is my second favorite principle, and it's quite simple. Scarcity is the fact that by making items or opportunities rarer, you make them more desirable. You're more likely to buy an item if it's rare and there are only a few pieces left. Retail owners know this and use it all the time, by lowering the price of a product for a limited amount of time.

Picture two people. One is searching for jobs all over the place, asking everyone if they have a job, and posting his resume to all the job applications he can get his hands on. Now contrast this with someone else who has four people looking at his resume, and want to hire him. Who do you think will get the better job position?

Obviously the second person, the professional who was able to position himself to be scarce, suddenly seems more desirable. Employers fight over him, competing with each other by offering raises and signing bonuses. This is why the hidden job market is a better place to be.

Further examples of scarcity in the workplace are employees getting several job offers, not being able to meet at all times, saying no to projects and new requests. The 10% do this all the time, precisely because they are in demand. Saying no allows them to work on their priorities and also to communicate to everyone that they're scarce, and hence valuable.

4 Magic Circles You Need To Master

Now that you know the six principles of influence, the question remains, whom do you influence in your organization?

I cover this in detail on my course. Instead of influencing everyone you can, which will be a waste of time and energy, you can instead focus your efforts on what I call the 4 Magic Circles. These are the people who, if you focus your efforts on, you'll be able to achieve your next job title in 10x less time.

HOW TO HAVE AN INFLUENTIAL PERSON BE YOUR MENTOR

Alright let's get down to one of the most important influence skills you'll learn, and that's how to get a very influential person to be your mentor.

You know exactly who I'm talking about, she's the person in your organization everyone talks about. When she gives the nod to any project or directive, it becomes company policy. She may not be the CEO or in senior management, but her opinion counts for a lot in your organization.

Obviously if you can enlist her as a mentor, your Career Acceleration will go a lot faster. Everyone will associate you with her, and it will influence your future boss to hire you.

On this subject, there's a lot of generic mentoring advice out there on the Internet. I call this "Blah Blah" advice because that's how it usually goes. This is what it "offers:"

Blah Blah Advice

- You need a mentor. *"Great"* you think, *"Awesome. I really didn't know that I need a mentor,"* and that's where the advice usually stops.
- Sometimes, maybe the advice goes to the next level of who you should choose as a mentor. That you should look at their skills and their position. That's great, but how do you start? Often this advice is ignored.

Leaving You With No Clarity

- Something these blog posts miss out on is that you should have one specific person to be your mentor. And they don't go about showing you how to get that person to be your mentor.
- Another piece of information they leave out is how you should approach mentors so that you can leverage them for the whole of your career. Not just for your next job promotion, but to develop a relationship that will last and thrive, even if you leave the organization. You want to create a relationship where both parties give to each other. Whether it's advice or valuable information. Often

these mentors turn into valuable friends after some time. That's what happens if you do this right.

If you choose the right person, this mentor will have the power to influence your future boss on their decision to hire you. Getting this person to be your mentor will be the shortcut required for your whole career, not just for your next job.

Once you enlist them, they'll be your champion, praising and evangelizing your brand when you need it.

I can't emphasize the benefits of this enough. Here are the top five hidden benefits of getting such a person to be your mentor:

- You will not only get your next job fast, but the job after that, and the job after that. Each time the process will be quick because each of your future bosses will listen to what your mentor has to say.
- Each of your bosses will be careful when interacting with you. Just this alone is powerful. You'll have respect, and everyone will know how to treat you.
- You'll develop a ton of social proof, fast. This is one of the six principles of influence, and you'll be able to use this social proof to get people on your side, whether it's for a project, or for a point of view.
- The financial and other perks are worth its weight in gold. Having an influential mentor will mean your name comes up whenever new stock is issued, or when bonuses are being written. You'll get access to VIP training and ride the career fast track.
- You'll grow professionally, fast. Having someone like this as a mentor will challenge how you think, forcing you to grow and to push your limits. You'll learn their way of thinking, which has taken them an entire career to learn and granted them the success they have. You'll gain a perspective that few can access.

Getting an influential mentor is more art than science. I'll illustrate this by sharing my story.

Back when I was a Brand Manager, the Brand Director was my boss. This was the position that I sought, and I knew that his boss, in turn, was the Head of Marketing. He would, in effect, be my hiring manager when I sought out that position.

I then sat down and thought to myself, *"Who is an influential person to the Head of Marketing? Who would my future boss listen to?"* The answer turned out to be the Head of Sales. He was a smart guy, very decisive, and an effective leader in the organization, leading 400 people. He was quite influential, and was all in all a brilliant mentor to have. He read tons and tons of books on strategy and leadership, but also applied everything that he learned. I knew that not only would he help me secure my next job, but would be an awesome mentor to have for the whole of my career.

So, how did I go about getting him as a mentor? After all, I was just a Junior Brand Manager, and he had greater than four hundred people to lead in his division.

I did something smart. I talked to my boss, a Brand Director at the time, and said something along the following, *"I'm looking to build these skills and behaviors. What do you think? Should I get a mentor? Do you know anyone who has these skills?"* My boss was at first quite hesitant, but I was prepared.
"What about the Head of Sales? He is exactly the right kind of person who has these skills and behaviors?" Of course I was mostly talking about the skills I wanted to learn, as opposed to how he could help me in my career.

My boss quickly agreed; he loved the idea. Why? Because he saw the benefit for himself. He saw it as a chance to get closer to the Head of Sales. He quickly made an introduction, and I enlisted the Head of Sales as a mentor. It was a phenomenal experience and I learned a lot.

That lasted for a year, and it changed quite a few things in my life. I got promoted in less than a year. Now, I wasn't promoted just because of this relationship, but it was an important factor when the conversation came up about who would be the next Brand Director.

Here's another example in my career. When I was Brand Director, I was looking at the next role I wanted, which was European Brand Director. This was a big leap up. I'd go from being responsible for a small country to being responsible for all of Europe. My current boss was the Marketing Head of the country, but my future boss was the Marketing Head of Europe. He was quite difficult to reach, but that didn't limit me. I stopped and thought to myself, *"Who does he find influential? Who would he listen to?"* I identified that he respected the opinion of one of the Marketing Heads of a country, so I reached out through my network to get that person to be my mentor.

Do you want to guess what happened as a result? After a year, I got a big bump from being a Brand Director of a small country to being promoted to a European Brand Director.

Not only that, but the story repeats itself in how I got promoted from European Brand Director to Global Product Director. Same principles. I found someone whose opinion my future boss valued, and enlisted them as a mentor.

This strategy is very powerful; it's one of the fastest techniques I've seen when it comes to career acceleration. Find someone your future boss finds influential, and get them to be your mentor. Use the mindset of the 10%, give value up front, and use the six principles of influence to bring them on board. Use any mentorship programs your organization may have as well if it's appropriate. If you can get the right person to be your mentor, you can get on the career fast track.

INFLUENCING FUTURE PEERS

I talk more about this in my course, but another group of people you should think about influencing are your future peers.

I mean, think about it for a second, your future peers are going to have a say to their boss on who gets the role. Why? Because your future boss worries about if the person will be a good fit, if they'll be liked by his team or not. Because if not, then no work will get done.

Let's see what Ordinary Joe does when he's dealing with future peers. The first time he meets them is when he's waiting for his job interview. Maybe they'll ask Joe if he wants a glass of water while he's waiting in the lobby. That's it; their sole interaction being a 30-second conversation. I can assure you in that amount of time, they don't have enough information to make a good judgment about Joe.

Or maybe Joe is more strategic. Maybe he's read an article in *Harvard Business Review* on how he needs to start influencing his future peers. So what does he do? He reaches out to them, but with the wrong mindset. He invites them for coffee, and what could have become a pleasant meeting suddenly becomes an interrogation. He asks this person, who he's never met before, *"So what are your plans? Are you moving to a new role? Are there any open positions for me?"* Joe is driven by a scarcity mindset, and all this does is harm his career more. His future peers have a negative impression of him, and you can be sure that when they're discussing with their boss the possibility of hiring him, they give a vehement *"No."*

Compare this with Extraordinary Jennifer. Jennifer is always seeking out ways to help people. She's already influential, so she gets a warm introduction to a few of her future peers. As they sit down for coffee, her future peers instantly like her, as she's a likeable person and knows how to warm up the conversation. All throughout she's constantly asking questions, which revolve around the theme of *"How can I help you?"*

When Jennifer is up for promotion, and her future boss asks her team what they think about Jennifer, what do you think they'll say?

That's the power of influencing your future peers.

INFLUENCE BEYOND THE WALLS OF YOUR COMPANY

You can learn more about this in my course, and for me, this is the next level for people to come back to once they've used influence to get onto the career fast track and have secured a few job promotions.

It's simple; with a certain set of strategies and tactics, you can achieve what I call "Ultimate Influence." This is when both external and internal recruiters and hiring managers are reaching out to you on a MONTHLY basis to hire you.

Can you imagine how powerful that is? To have job offers arriving in your inbox on a monthly basis? Imagine the negotiating power that would give you in your organization. Or maybe they don't reach out with job offers, but to consult you about someone or something else. This is also powerful, this can give you a ton of social proof, and it'll be on autopilot. This is the *ultimate influence.*

If you want more help getting this level and power of influence, get your free bonus cheat sheet here: www.career10x.com/bonuses. This is usually only available to my personal coaching students, but it's so valuable in your career acceleration, that I want to gift it to you.

To Summarize:

- Influence is the number one skill you can use to rapidly accelerate your career, and is the most important ability you can learn for success, no matter your field.
- The 90% engage in "Cover Your Ass" activities, also known as office politics, to seek certainty. The 10% use authenticity and influence to recruit people to their point of view. They're willing to stand behind their ideas even if they're controversial, as they know that being safe is risky.
- There are six principles of influence: Reciprocity, Consistency, Social Proof, Likeability, Authority, and Scarcity.
- Getting a mentor who has influence over your future boss is one of the most dramatic ways to accelerate you to your next job promotion.
- Recruiting your future peers to your side is something that's also critical to your success.

CONCLUSION

Congratulations on reaching this point of the book. No, really, you've earned it. You're serious about our career. You're serious about entering the 10% club.

I put this book, this strategy together, because when I was struggling in my career, specifically with my first two jobs, I was overwhelmed with all the information that was out there on the subject. I wanted to advance in my career, but I couldn't find a clear, step-by-step strategy on how to achieve that. Most of the advice I could find that promised something similar was just plain wrong. There were books that offered tips on how to craft my resume and how to write a cover letter, or on how to impress my boss and speak his language... but nothing that would offer a step-by-step system for career advancement.

Aware of this, I decided to take a different approach. I studied success and I experimented with my own approach. I was bold enough to test out things that others would be afraid of even thinking about.

As I applied what I learned, threw out what didn't work, and kept what did, I started to experience rapid acceleration in my career, as you now know. But it was only when others started asking me for advice that I started formalizing what I've learned. I remember the months where my calendar was fully booked with mentoring sessions. I was obsessed with finding out the right way to teach what I know. Slowly, over time, I started putting together my Career Acceleration Formula. A 6-step strategy that's based on timeless principles.

I'm confident that my Career Acceleration Formula will work for you, not just because it's based on my own experience and the experience of other successful people, but because I've helped hundreds of students experience rapid career acceleration, too. These strategies are timeless. They worked a hundred years ago, and they will work for many decades to come.

So just to recap, here's the six steps of the Career Acceleration Formula.

THE 6 STEPS OF THE CAREER ACCELERATION FORMULA

Career Acceleration = Mindset x Value x Leverage.

Step 1: Mindset

Before you start, you have to adopt the mindset of the 10%, you have to find out what's holding you back in the invisible world, and get it working for you.

They are:

- Value first (or "How can I help?").
- I am the product.
- I work smart, not hard.
- Career success is in my hands (or "I am in charge and can control it").
- Success patterns are learnable.
- Best jobs aren't advertised; they're created for the best people.
- The Compound Effect is the most powerful force in nature.
- Having a great career is *fun*.

Step 2: Choose Your Perfect Next Job Title

A perfect career consists of a series of perfect jobs. It's that simple. That doesn't mean it's easy. You need to make sure that your next job title is the *right* job title, not just aligned with your strengths, but the kind of job title that will get you noticed and has the opportunity for you to deliver huge impact to your organization. Because of this, the three critical elements of your perfect job title are:

- Playing the right game.
- Knowing your strengths, and playing to them.
- Knowing your competitive advantage.

Once you have some ideas on your next job title, you have to get feedback from others, ideally from people who have had that job title. If there are any red flags, move on to your next job title. It's okay for this part to take some time. This process can take anywhere from two weeks to two months. And that's okay, because if you get this right, your chances of your career accelerating become greater.

Step 3: Your One Big Thing

This is where we really enter the Value element of the Career Acceleration Formula. Your One Big Thing is your flagship project, the one thing you concentrate on because you know it will deliver 10x results to your organization and your career. It's your Eiffel Tower, your Mona Lisa, your Sistine Chapel... for the next 6-12 months. It can take you up to three months to identify your One Big Thing, but it's worth it. Because having a One Big Thing allows you to prioritize. You can say no to other projects with confidence, and other people in your organization will respect you for it. I recommend to my students to work on their One Big Thing for one hour at the start of their work day, before they check email or work on anything else. This way you're keeping your personal career goals above your company's goals, and you'll create momentum and feel in charge of your career.

You'll also deliver more value to your organization as a result. Win-win.

Step 4: Make Your Boss Work For You

This is where you start to get leverage in your career acceleration. If done right, you can make your boss your secret supporter throughout your career. You can use simple strategies from psychology to secure the help from your boss in climbing to the next step up in your career. And guess what? Your boss wants to do it! He wants you to advance in your career. He wants you to achieve your goals. All you have to do is win him over to your side.

Step 5: You 2.0

There's a fundamental difference between how the 10% club and the 90% crowd approach their next job title. The 90% view their next promotion as them *getting* their next job title. The 10% *grow* into their next job title. Once you've identified your perfect next job title, and won your boss over to your side, it's time to start focusing on your growth. Carry out a 360 Degree Feedback survey to find out what others think of your strengths and limitations. Then gain clarity on what You 2.0 will look like, make sure your next destination is perfect for not just the long term, but for the short term in your career. Finally, carry out a simulation project to address any objections your future boss may have about you.

Step 6: Become The Center Of Influence.

This is the final piece of the puzzle, and it's how to get maximum leverage for your career. Influence is the number one skill you'll need in your working life. Even if you leave the corporate world and decide to start a business, or enter into the nonprofit world, you'll still need influence to succeed. Here you learned about the six principles of influence. You also learned how to get a mentor to accelerate your career and how to influence your future peers and your future boss. I guarantee you once you start applying this step, coupled with the other steps, you'll experience career acceleration like you've never had before.

YOUR TURN

So that's the Career Acceleration Formula. Now it's your turn. You've seen the case studies; you know what's possible. You know how to enter the 10% club. You know how to upgrade your career on demand.

All of my personal success comes down to what I've shown in this book. This is the exact step-by-step strategy that I've used to get promoted six times in six years with a 15x bump in salary. More importantly, it's the strategy I've helped hundreds of students use to get promoted in 6-12 months in such Fortune 500 companies as Google, JP Morgan, Ralph Lauren, Accenture, Ford, SAP, IBM, J&J and many, many others. My students sometimes say that my Career Acceleration Formula has become a secret weapon of the ambitious Fortune 500 professional. The Career Acceleration Formula works, and now it's your turn to use it.

Throughout this book I've referenced a collection of free career acceleration resources I created for you. These free resources will help you maximise what you learned in this book and shortcut the journey to your next promotion, you can get them all by visiting: www.career10x.com/bonuses

However, you have to start taking action. It's up to you whether you can enter the 10% club. You have the strategy in your hands, you know how to get onto the career fast track, and you know success is possible.

Trust me, getting into the 10% club is worth it. I'll share with you a brief story why.

A STORY I KEPT FOR THE VERY END

As I said before, after I went from being an entry level underpaid Sales Representative to becoming a Global Product Director managing a portfolio worth $5 Billion in just a handful of years, people started to notice. I was mentoring as many people as I could; my calendar was packed with meetings day after day.

Based on my own success and that of my students, I knew I was on to something. I realized this information was valuable and could help lots of people around the world get the success they always wanted. But I didn't know how to get the word out.

Around this time, in December 2012, I attended Tony Robbins' Date With Destiny seminar, and my mind was blown. It cost $5,000 just to attend, but it was worth it. I realized that I needed to take some time to regroup, and think about my career and my life from a different perspective. Carl Jung refers to this phase as Individuation, and Wayne Dyer calls it *The Shift*. It's part of everyone's personal growth. It was time for me to find out what I really wanted. I also wanted to put everything I'd learned about career acceleration into a format that could reach everyone in the world.

A month later I attended a seminar in London, where I learned how to use technology to share my message with the world. Instead of going around mentoring people one by one, I could put together an online course and reach people all across the world.

Here's the thing, I truly believe in the power of education to change the world. Sometimes when I start thinking about the potential education has to make the world a better place, it gives me shivers, and I can't contain my excitement. Today, a child in Uganda with a laptop has access to information that the President of the United States did 20 years ago.

I knew what I had to do. I decided I was going to take a sabbatical year off. The sabbatical was going to have three goals: travel and explore a part of the world, personal development, and regrouping and launching an online course to help people with their careers.

Here's the thing, the moment I started talking about my plans to take a sabbatical year off, I started getting a lot of discouragement.

"Bozi, that's not a wise idea. Your company won't forgive you."

"Bozi... that's career suicide. Why stop the momentum you've built up?"

"Bozi I don't think people will appreciate you taking time off..."

But I'd received comments like this throughout my career. Whenever I attempted something uncommon, I would get advice that reflects common thinking. I paused and thought about all the advice I was getting. Why were they going out of their way to discourage me from my sabbatical?

Well first, and I know this may sound harsh, but I think they were secretly jealous. Many people want to take a sabbatical but they're afraid. They're afraid that a year off will kill their careers, so they rationalize to themselves that sabbaticals are a bad idea. Second, this stemmed from 90% thinking, which is to not rock the boat, to not stand out, to not do anything that seems too rash. But as I have shown you, this thinking is a guaranteed way to kill your career. If you want uncommon results, you have to take uncommon actions. It's that simple.

Finally, it was *the perception* of taking a sabbatical year off that was a threat. Not the actual consequences. I sat down and asked myself, what was the worst-case scenario of taking a year off? Okay, I won't get my job back. Would it be possible to get a new job? Of course. I had the confidence and experience to get a different job if it came down to it.

So I let my company know about my plan for the following year. When they asked why, I told them my goals: to travel and explore, take some time for personal development, and to launch an online course to help people with their careers. Most people would advise that you should hide your entrepreneurial pursuits. Again this is common thinking.

It turns out my bosses were happy with this. Ever since that seminar in London, I'd been teaching myself the principles of digital marketing, and pursuing it on the side. It was my hobby during the evening and the weekends. My bosses liked the fact I was teaching myself new skills, and exercising my entrepreneurial muscles. Why? Because they knew that it could be of value to the organization.

So I took a year off. I travelled to Southeast Asia and had an unforgettable experience. During this time, I looked through my notes on career acceleration and started to put together a strategy and an outline for an online course.

I won't lie... it took some time to find something that works. There were a few false starts and failed projects, but six months later, Career Acceleration Formula was born.

And I was blown away by the results. It got picked up by the Huffington Post and IvyExec, and started to attract people from companies such as Google, Oracle, JP Morgan, Ralph Lauren,

Ford... companies with professionals I never thought I'd be able to reach.

And here's the thing, when I returned from my sabbatical, I had perfect clarity on what I wanted my next role to be. I went back to the executive team of my company and asked for a global leadership role at the intersection of healthcare, business and, you guessed it, digital, and a relocation to New York.

It turned out that while I was away, my company was going through a rapid change exactly to adapt to becoming more digital. Suddenly, they needed people with strong experience in my field, proven business acumen (launching new products), and hands on expertise with digital marketing. And they couldn't find the right fit. They needed people to lead this new division, and since it was uncharted territory, they needed someone entrepreneurial. It was almost like the position was tailor-made for me. Here was a role that would allow me to exercise my digital skills, and use the entrepreneurial muscles I'd developed during my year off.

After several rounds of interviews (in which I used my formula of course), I got the role I wanted, coupled with a New York relocation package, a gorgeous office on the 50th floor with an amazing view of the city, an almost blank check to form my new team, and an opportunity to lead one of the most exciting projects in a $60 Billion per year Fortune 500 company.

Oh and guess what? I got a 22% increase in total compensation, with my housing costs being fully covered by the company.

Stop and think about that for a second. I took a year off, something that's considered career suicide, pursued my own thing, came back, asked for a very specific role (my Perfect Next Job) and got that new role with 22% more money and my housing costs paid.

Uncommon actions lead to uncommon results.

Why am I sharing this story? Because I wanted you to realize why you need to enter the 10% club. If I were still in the 90% crowd, chasing promotions through traditional job applications, I would never have had the confidence to take a year off and find out what I truly wanted to do. I wouldn't have the life satisfaction I have now of helping people get the success they've always wanted in their careers. I wouldn't have had the opportunity to marry my interests of digital marketing to my current role.

By entering the 10% club, you'll have the greatest opportunity, the greatest platform, to bring your best self to the world. To finally start implementing the change you want to see in the world. It can be something as simple as pursuing that side project that will inspire others, or of instituting a change in your organization that will change the world.

The choice is up to you.

Where Do You Go From Here?

First of all - thank you for reading Promoted. I appreciate you more than I can say here, and if just one of the strategies you discovered in this book helps you, I'll consider my job well done.

Now, if you're looking to take the lessons inside Promoted and get step-by-step training from me, I suggest you attend one of my free online training sessions. You can visit the link below to find out more details and see when my next free training is:

www.career10x.com/free-training

To your career success,

Bozi Dar

Use this book. Use the bonus material provided for you. Take the first steps to enter the 10% club. And when you do, send me your story at <u>bozidar@career10x.com</u>. There's nothing better in the world for me than hearing about someone else's success story in their career, about getting the life satisfaction they've always wanted.

I'll see you on the other side. On the side of the 10% club.